Made For This Moment

Our Time, Our Life, Our Legacy

CONNIE FRIEND

authorHOUSE®

AuthorHouse™
1663 Liberty Drive
Bloomington, IN 47403
www.authorhouse.com
Phone: 1-800-839-8640

Published by AuthorHouse 7/23/2012

ISBN: 978-1-4772-4457-9 (sc)
ISBN: 978-1-4772-4456-2 (e)

Library of Congress Control Number: 2012912416

Contents

Acknowledgments

THIS BOOK is not the singular work of me alone. Many people have helped shape my beliefs, my passion, and who I have become as a person. I want to thank those who have collaborated and contributed to this effort.

- My husband, Stan, for being my partner, my coach, my cheerleader, and my lover for 28 years. He is not afraid to challenge me and he makes me better. As a pastor, he is making a significant, lasting impact for the Kingdom. He also reminds me to breathe fresh air once in a while. He was made for this moment.

- My three children, Tyler, Alyssa, and Greyson. I never would have imagined that my most important mission field would become my most valuable missionaries. They help me, bless me, and encourage me every day. I'm so proud of who they are. They were made for this moment.

- My parents, Reg and Pat. They have always offered me support and unconditional love.

They sacrificed to move their family forward. They were made for this moment.

- My editors (who are also my friends), Sheri Irwin, Susan Sorenson, Brenda Simpson Sandquist, Aly Friend, Brenna Bell, and Melanie Simmons. They have encouraged me and fixed all my problems. They were made for this moment.

- My friends (who are also my storytellers), Alejandra Hernandez, Sue Musselman, Sheri Irwin, Brenda Simpson Sandquist, Jean Higgins, and Gere' Clark. They are brave and vulnerable in telling their stories and they are helping many people. They were made for this moment.

- The Women of Our Time. They are always up for an adventure. They have taken this journey with me and they make it so fun to do life together. They inspire me. They were made for this moment.

- The People of Capital Christian Center, Carson City, NV. They have loved me and given me room to grow. God has lit them on fire and people are coming from miles around to watch them burn. They were made for this moment.

My Legacy

Introduction

Made For This Moment
Our Time. Our Life. Our Legacy.

I BELIEVE THAT every person is born with a measure of faith and with a unique destiny to fulfill. God's desire is that we rise up, stand to our full stature in Him, and accomplish whatever he has put within our hearts to do.

I have worked to mentor, train, and encourage people for many years, and every week I encounter at least one dear woman who is in the middle of a battle. The battle is always something that terrifies her and threatens all she knows to be true. It may be a husband who is not willing to surrender to God and whose addictions have got her on the verge of losing hope; she feels like she can't hold on any longer. It may be a serious illness she is facing, and she would rather just pack it all in and give up because the battle is too hard. It may be the death of a family member that makes her question why God would allow such a thing to happen to her and now the most difficult thing in the world for her to do is to continue breathing in and out.

I want to tell you now what I have told them. The

challenge you are facing is big, but it's not bigger than our God, and it's not stronger than His Spirit that resides within you. God created you, He prepared you, and He will sustain you through the fight. You may not feel like it, and you may not even believe me as you read these words, but you were made for this moment.

Beyond Bravery

I stepped onto the parking lot and watched my twenty-one year old son drive my husband's beautiful Harley Davidson motorcycle for the first time. No classes, no instructions, he just got on and rode. It looked EASY!

I was feeling bold. I was feeling empowered. I was feeling capable and strong.

As he pulled up to me, I strapped on my helmet and traded places with him. I was so ready! My husband tried to patiently show me where the brakes were, where the gears were, and where the throttle was. I sat on the hog and took off.

Within a few seconds, I realized how heavy that bike was. I tried to steer it, I tried to turn it, but it wouldn't budge. My mind was whirling, trying to problem solve as I rode, I couldn't remember which thingy was which.

"How do I stop?" "How do I slow down?" I knew I was in trouble.

I was headed straight for a parking lot planter island. In the planter, I knew there was a fire hydrant, a light pole, a gas line, and a few trees. Since I couldn't turn the bike, I knew that's where I was going.

As I approached the island, I tried to stop but I confused the brake with the throttle, and as the engine roared, my front tire hit the curb. I felt myself go through a tree limb, hit and bust through the windshield, and be tossed into the air. I just wanted to stop moving!

I blacked out.

The first thing I remember was hearing the footsteps of my son as he frantically ran toward me. I was very still. Afraid to move. Afraid to lift my face from the pavement, afraid of finding out what damage I had done. I rolled over, and by then my son, my husband and friends were standing over me. "Do I still have teeth?" I asked. My husband's voice was extraordinarily kind and gentle, so I knew I must've looked bad. "Your teeth are ok, you're just a little scraped up" he said.

After a few minutes, I got up off the pavement, gingerly climbed into a car and went to the emergency room. As they examined me, they found large contusions covering my body, scrapes, hematomas developing, sprained thumbs, and two broken bones in my toe. It could've been a lot worse. I was very lucky.

The bike didn't fare any better. It still needs some repairs, it drives crooked, and some of the beautiful chrome got scraped off. It will be awhile before it's drivable again. A split second of insanity can turn into months of regret.

What happened? I was feeling so strong, yet with one decision, with thundering stupidity, my fearlessness was stripped away and I was left battered, bruised and in need of a lengthy recovery. Why? Because boldness without wisdom is just plain dangerous! I should have taken a motorcycle safety class. I should have gained instruction, but I thought my bravery was enough.

Navigating life can be tricky. Sometimes our senses deceive us; what we see and what we hear do not completely line up with the questions we encounter. We hear the old saying, "No guts, no glory," ringing in our ears, so we muster strength and tell ourselves we can do it. Some of our friends make it look easy and just by watching them, we are tempted to think that fortitude will be enough to get us through the challenges of life successfully. It takes more than boldness and it takes more than bravery to live a successful life. My crash is living proof that boldness is not enough.

Wisdom Behind Your Boldness

My purpose in writing this book is to help put wisdom behind your boldness that will propel you to victory in every circumstance you face.

In the book of Job, he utters sentiments that I have often felt as I have grown in my relationship with God.

> *"How you have helped the powerless!*
> *How you have saved the weak!*
> *How you have enlightened my stupidity!*
> *What wise advice you have offered!"*
> Job 26:2-3 (NLT)

Maybe you can relate to that. There are times in life when we just need a little help. We too, go through circumstances that make us feel powerless, weak, and maybe even stupid. We experience moments when things are great and we're on top of the world but we also go through times of fear, sadness, sorrow, pain, loneliness, and frustration. We can allow these moments to define us, or we can choose to rise and let them simply refine us.

Like my motorcycle incident, most of the time, we would not WANT a moment like that to happen. But moments like that do happen, to all of us. Maybe for you, it happened in the midst of a tragedy. Someone dear to you passed away and all the people turned to see how you would cope. Possibly you are placed in the middle of a battle you didn't choose, like cancer or illness. People don't have the right words to say, so they stand back and watch you to see how you handle it. What will your next choice be? How will you manage? Maybe it's a loss of a job, or better yet, maybe you are facing great success and a promotion comes your way. The big moments in life aren't always bad.

Maybe you haven't come to your moment yet. But you will.

Defining moments have a way of sneaking up on us. The big moments come upon us suddenly when we least expect them, and in that instant we realize with every breath, that *this moment* is laden with potential. *This moment* carries the potential to thrust us into our future and alter the destiny of our entire legacy. It comes down to our perspective, our ownership and many times, our courage. *This moment* offers us a choice to either be the victim or to be the victor of our own story.

In the following chapters it is my desire to help offer you a fresh perspective that will put you in position to see your situation as God might see it. I also want to put tools in your hands that will encourage you to accept responsibility for your moment and to rise to your full potential as God's beautiful daughter. We will explore stories from the Bible, from history, and from women in my world that might offer you the right dose of courage to rise.

This will be a unique six week journey that gives you one chapter of reading each weekend then provides a personal devotion experience the other five days of the week.

In Joel 3:10, the prophet was rallying the people, and the words that encouraged them in their terrifying moment of battle, encourage us still. *"Let the weak say, I am strong."* (NIV)

God would not tell us to be strong if we didn't have it in us to be strong. He tells us to simply be what He has already made us to be. He is always calling us to a higher level, to stop living beneath our privileges as His child and to come up to a better place. I believe that *this moment* can push us into a greater destiny than we could ever dream of.

Joel goes on to say, a few verses later, *"Thousands upon*

thousands are waiting in the valley of decision. There the day of the Lord will soon arrive. " Joel 3:14 (NLT)

Maybe that verse describes you right now. You may have countless thousands waiting in your future who need what you have to offer, who may depend upon your wisdom. It is time to stop thinking you can't do it and that *this moment* is too much for you to handle. It's not too much! It's time to stop waiting! It's not beyond the scope of God's plan for your life. This is it! It's time to get prepared. It's time to gain wisdom. It's time for you to be bold. You were made for this moment!

Chapter 1
Made For More

"To EVERYTHING *there is a season, and a time for every matter or purpose under heaven: A time to be born and a time to die, a time to plant and a time to pluck up what is planted"* Ecclesiastes 3:1-2 (AMP)

Gianna Jessen, a beautiful, articulate young woman, stood before the Constitution Subcommittee of the House Judiciary Committee on April 22, 1996. This is her testimony.

"My name is Gianna Jessen. I am nineteen years of age. I am originally from California, but now reside in Franklin, Tennessee. I am adopted. I have cerebral palsy. My biological mother was 17 years old and seven and one-half months pregnant when she made the decision to have a saline abortion. I am the person she aborted. I lived instead of died.

Fortunately for me the abortionist was not in the clinic when I arrived alive, instead of dead, at 6:00 a.m. on the morning of April 6, 1977. I was early, my death was not expected to be seen until about 9 a.m., when he would probably be arriving for his office hours. I am sure I would

1

not be here today if the abortionist would have been in the clinic as his job is to take life, not sustain it. Some have said I am a 'botched abortion', a result of a job not well done.

There were many witnesses to my entry into this world. My biological mother and other young girls in the clinic, who also awaited the death of their babies, were the first to greet me. I am told this was a hysterical moment. Next was a staff nurse who apparently called emergency medical services and had me transferred to a hospital.

I remained in the hospital for almost three months. There was not much hope for me in the beginning. I weighed only two pounds. Today, babies smaller than I was have survived.

A doctor once said I had a great will to live and that I fought for my life. I eventually was able to leave the hospital and be placed in foster care. I was diagnosed with cerebral palsy as a result of the abortion...

I am happy to be alive. I almost died. Every day I thank God for life. I do not consider myself a by-product of conception, a clump of tissue, or any other of the titles given to a child in the womb. I do not consider any person conceived to be any of those things...

All life is valuable. All life is a gift from our Creator. We must receive and cherish the gifts we are given. We must honor the right to life."[1]

Gianna Jessen expresses courage every day of her life. She is walking, talking, living, breathing, evidence that God creates us with purpose.

You were created with a purpose as well. By virtue of your birth, you have proof that you are destined to fill a place in history. There's no denying it. You are here, and nothing can erase the fact that you have existed. You didn't choose it, you didn't ask for your place of origin or condition of birth, you had no control over it, but still, you are here. You were specifically created by a loving God with a plan.

Breath of God

You are breathing. You have the very breath of God in your lungs. When God created human kind, he finished his masterpiece by breathing His very own spirit, (in Greek, the word is "pneuma" which means breath[2]) into us from His own being. Stop and take in that thought for a moment. The holy breath of God is within you! It is sacred. It is holy. It is powerful. The fact that you are breathing in and out right now as you read this, means you have supernatural, holy, sacred potential residing within you.

When Moses asked God His name, God responded with the word Yahweh, which translates, "I am who I am." The word Yahweh is composed of the Hebrew letters, YHWH. These letters coupled with the appropriate vowels sounds imitate the sound of breathing. In both Hebrew and Greek, the word for spirit is the same as the word for breath.[3] Our God is present in all things, and our God is present in us.

When a newborn infant draws their first breath, they speak the name of God. Yahweh. When a person on their deathbed draws their last breath, the name of God is on their lips. Yahweh. Even those who say there is no God speak His name of the very act of breathing. Yahweh.

Jason Gray wrote lyrics to a beautiful song that depicts the breath of God upon us.

"The Sound of Our Breathing"

"Every one of us is born of dust
but come alive with heaven's kiss

> The name of God is the sound of our breathing
> Hallelujahs rise on the wings of our hearts beating"[4]

God created you and breathed His own divine breath and life into you. This is your time, and this moment will never pass again.

Precious Moments

In contrast to Gianna's story, my story seems rather insignificant but that is precisely the point. None of us are insignificant. Each one of us is precious, planned for, and purposed by God.

From Wandering to Wondering

What are you going to do with the time you've been given? That is the question I began asking about the time I turned forty. I began wondering what I was going to do with the rest of my life. Sadly, I realized my life was probably half over. Would the second half be better than the first half? Was it going to matter to anyone that I was here? And even more importantly, was I going to do anything to make a difference in someone else's life?

I had been studying the book of Exodus in the Bible about that time. The striking comparison was hard to miss;

the children of Israel, though they belonged to God, had wandered and wasted forty years. I was feeling like my life was wasting away as well. After my 40th birthday, I realized I was experiencing such a deep feeling of dissatisfaction. I had an epiphany. I suddenly realized that all my life I had been overwhelmed with a feeling of shyness, a lack of confidence, and lethargy of purpose, and I was not willing to wander in the desert one more day!

I think this feeling hits different people at different points throughout life. John Mayer wrote about it in his song, "Why Georgia."[5] A quarter life crisis can be a very real and challenging event in young people too. Some experience it as they finish high school or college. Others experience this kind of crisis while waiting to get married or waiting to have children. For others it's while going through a divorce or a demise of a dream or a death of a loved one. It doesn't always hit you at mid-life, or when you're 40. I've had friends go through similar experiences even in their 80's. It is a universal part of life, but this stress and fear of stagnation can actually keep us growing and moving forward.

A Point of Reference

We all go through times in our lives when we wonder "Why was I born?" and "Why am I here?" and "What is my purpose?" Rick Warren jumpstarted a huge discussion in our culture when he wrote his best seller, *The Purpose Driven Life*.[6] He launched his career, expanded his church, and opened fresh dialogue across the American landscape. The book sought to answer these very important questions we face. In it he states, "But there is a God who made you for a reason, and your life has profound meaning! We discover that meaning and purpose only when we make God the reference point of our lives."

Is God the reference point of your life? How do you know?

My children are nearly grown now, and I'm beginning to see the fruits of my investment and of pouring my life into theirs, which is a wonderful thing for any parent. I don't negate the value of motherhood, or the investment that I poured into the life of my family for a second. My search for deeper meaning did not negate the amazing gift my family has been in my life, I just mean that at some level, I wanted more.

Groundhog Day

I vividly remember when my children were young and every day felt like a scene from the movie *Groundhog Day*. I would wake up every morning feeling exhausted, only to repeat the same tasks and chores of the day before, feeling caught in the cycle of daily maintenance routines and constant care of little ones. "Wash, rinse, repeat. Wash, rinse, repeat." Have you ever felt like this?

I remember occasionally looking in the mirror, seeing fatigue on my face, burnout in my eyes, and frequently, a serious case of bed head, saying to myself in dismay, "Woman, who are you, and how did you get here?"

As my kids began physically needing me less and less, it gave me time to start asking the question, "Is this all there is?" I began feeling that I just wanted more even if I didn't know what more was.

Driven

To begin answering any of those questions, I had to realize who I was. This search led me on a quest that began in 2004. I felt driven to find answers, driven to my knees, and driven to change. Appropriately, I began reading *Purpose Driven Life*. I took notes and I did some sincere introspection and analysis.

In 2005, I was able to go to the Hillsong Conference, put on by Hillsong Church in Sydney, Australia. While in Australia, I saw modeled before me women who knew and understood that they had a responsibility as the female half of God's church, to BE the church. I caught a real glimpse, for the first time, that I too was intended for a purpose.

I listened to one of the women on staff at their church, Pastor Donna Crouch. She told the story of finding Jesus and beginning to work at the church. She told of her growth and evolution from shy girl in the background to a leader of multitudes. She began speaking out all the excuses I had in the running commentary in my head. There were so many reasons why I wouldn't do anything for God, did not take risks, could not speak up. I couldn't tolerate the mess of failure, or the loss of control. She said things like, "So you're not qualified. Get qualified!" A statement that hit me right between the eyes... Get qualified...

Did you know that the Bible is completely full of God's thoughts about you? I once attended a prophetic worship class, not knowing at all what that title meant. The teacher said, "Just start worshiping and praying, and begin stating what God says about you."

"What does God say about you?" the teacher asked. I must confess, I was stumped. At that time in my life, I was clueless. I mean, I knew that Jesus died on the cross to save human kind, and I was one of those, but what did He think of me personally? I wasn't sure.

So I came home and began to research what God thinks and I started to devour the Word of God. I was blown away by what I found.

He says we are complete. *"So you also are complete through your union with Christ, who is the head over every ruler and authority."* Colossians 2:10 (NLT)

He says we are saved and called. *"For God saved us and called us to live a holy life. He did this, not because we deserved it, but because that was his plan from the beginning of time - to show us his grace through Christ Jesus."* 2 Timothy 1:9 (NLT)

He says we are guarded and loved. *"He found them in a desert land, in an empty, howling wasteland. He surrounded them and watched over them; he guarded them as he would guard his own eyes."* Deuteronomy 32:10 (NLT)

He says we are loved. *"Even before he made the world, God loved us and chose us in Christ to be holy and without fault in his eyes."* Ephesians 1:4 (NLT)

He says we are blessed, happy and favored. *"So then, those who are people of faith are blessed and made happy and favored by God [as a partner in fellowship] with the believing and trusting Abraham."* Galatians 3:9 (Amplified)

He says we are victorious. *"No, despite all these things, overwhelming victory is ours through Christ, who loved us."* Romans 8:37 (NLT)

He says we are beautiful. *"He has made everything beautiful in its time. He also has planted eternity in men's hearts and minds [a divinely implanted sense of a purpose working through the ages which nothing under the sun but God alone can satisfy], yet so that men cannot find out what God has done from the beginning to the end."* Ecclesiastes 3:11 (Amplified)

Complete, saved, called, guarded, loved, blessed, happy, favored, victorious and beautiful! Wow! How much more evidence do we need to realize He is head over heels, crazy about us?!

The Love Letter

When I began reading and understanding God's Word as a love letter to me, my whole perspective began to change. I began to look for the things God was doing. I started to realize that I didn't have to reinvent the wheel or find some magical potion that would complete me and add meaning to my life. I also began to comprehend that I already had everything I needed to be His girl.

God had already been working, placing things within my hands, within my sphere of influence and my realm of responsibility. I no longer had to wait for the perfect time. This was it!

I started realizing what Jesus meant when He said, *"I have come that they may have life, and that they may have it to the full."* John 10:10 (NIV) A full life. Not a routine, not drudgery, not a hold-your-breath-and-get-through-it kind of existence? I wanted it. I looked for it. I began reading God's Word more, letting Him breathe His life into me once again. I began reading other books by authors who were full of passion and zeal. I surrounded myself with people going in the same direction I was going.

Committed to the Journey

I actually didn't know where I was going, but that wasn't as important as being committed to the journey. I began to see that I didn't have to justify my existence or feel guilty for taking up space because I had a reason for being here. God gave me breath for a reason, and I no longer had to wait for permission to speak.

Perhaps you too have found yourself waiting in the wings for any number of reasons. Perhaps circumstances just seem too difficult. Maybe you have been taking care of others for years, and there's no time left to even consider your own calling. It could be that you think your past is too terrible to overcome. The weight of the guilt you carry is so heavy you think God wouldn't (or couldn't) use you. If the guilt and shame weren't enough of a burden, you wouldn't want to submit yourself to the scrutiny or the attention that comes from being in the forefront and the pressure of everyone "seeing" you. Standing on the edge of stepping out is an intimidating place to be.

We were created with great purpose, skill and intentionality. We have been watched for and waited on. We all have a certain amount of time allotted to us. We all have a certain number of days scheduled for us in this life. We can waste our time or we can spend it, but we cannot save a single day by waiting. God is able to give us more. He delights in making us into more. Stop doubting and know that you were made for this moment.

> *"Now to him who is able to do immeasurably more than all we ask or imagine, according to his power that is at work within us."* Ephesians 3:20 (NIV)

"Our deepest fear is not that we are inadequate. Our deepest fear is that we are powerful beyond measure. It is our light, not our darkness, that frightens us most. We ask ourselves, 'Who am I to be brilliant, gorgeous, talented, and famous?' Actually, who are you not to be? You are a child of God. Your playing small does not serve the world. There is nothing enlightened about shrinking so that people won't feel insecure around you. We were born to make manifest the glory of God that is within us. It's not just in some of us; it's in all of us. And when we let our own light shine, we unconsciously give other people permission to do the same. As we are liberated from our own fear, our presence automatically liberates others."
Maryanne Williamson[7]

Ale's Story
In Her Own Words

I was born January 16, 1988 in Mexico City. I came to America in January, 1990 with my mom, my 8 year old brother and my 10 year old sister when I was 2 years old. I grew up with a lot of love but lacked attention. From as long as I can remember my parents were always gone. They worked so much, and it was not unusual for them to work through the weekend including Sundays. They worked overlapping shifts so that we were never all home together as a family.

When I started school I did not know any English, so I remember coloring a lot and not having many friends. I graduated from ESL (English as a Second Language) in the third grade and also received my citizenship and my first F in school that year. When my mom changed jobs, she began working from 3pm to 12am, and that dramatically changed my outlook on life.

I was 8 when my sister was 16. She always had friends over and locked me in my room. She would go to parties and lock me in the car for hours at a time by myself and then threaten me later not to tell my parents. I wanted her to like me so I never told on her but the longer I was abandoned in cars or in my room, the more I felt like I was just in the way. I started losing my value during those years. My family was too busy for me so I turned to friends. I met two friends when I was in sixth grade and we became best friends. I felt like I finally fit in. We dressed in matching colors, spent every recess together and talked on the phone after school. We were pretty popular. My mom was very strict and never let me hang out with friends or have sleepovers after school though. I loved to run and play sports and it was the only thing my mom allowed me to do after school. I was running for Silver State Striders, an after school running program, every day until about 7pm.

One of my friends had a brother that was in a gang and he picked her up from school every day with his friends, which part of me thought it was scary, and the other part thought it pretty was cool. I was invited on a Friday to hang out with my friend at her house because she said she would be home alone, but I said I couldn't because of practice and my mom wouldn't let me. But she insisted and started teasing me. I was afraid not to be accepted by her anymore, so I decided to go to her house instead of practice after school. As long as I was home by 7pm I thought I could get away with it.

I went over to her house which was just a couple of blocks from my house but her brother was home waiting for us. He said he needed to go somewhere to drop something off. I didn't want want to go but I also couldn't go home because my mom would find out that I didn't go to practice and that privilege would get taken away from me, I felt stuck. He promised he would be quick and have me back by 7pm. I knew in my heart and in the pit of my stomach that I should not go but I did. He took us to a hotel and told us to get out. He insisted he would be quick. When he opened the door to the hotel room I noticed one of my brothers friends was there and it scared me so I ran into the bathroom and hid. All I wanted was to go home. I didn't care about anything else, but he told me to calm down and that we were almost ready to leave, then he gave me something to drink.

All I remember after that is in pieces, mostly auditory things. I remember being carried out of the hotel and laid on peoples laps in the truck. I felt so sick and they were touching me everywhere. We arrived at a different place and I think a party was going on because it was so loud there. I was carried into a room with bunk beds because I remember seeing the railing above me. I remember there was a huge fight. Two or three girls were yelling at the guys who brought me there and they even threatened to call the cops but they were kicked out.

There were 8 to 12 guys total, some I knew, others I did not. By the grace of God, I don't remember and didn't feel a lot of what happened to me next. I remember voices in my ear but I don't remember the words. I woke up once during the night and felt cold. It was then that I realized that I was cold because I was completely naked. Someone came into the room and saw that I was awake and freaked out. They made me drink something again. They began freaking out. They thought I had stopped breathing and were attempting CPR and discussing dropping me off outside the hospital.

I woke up the next morning on the floor in a completely different place surrounded by people sleeping. I didn't know anyone except one person. Next to me was a camcorder that was on pause. It just didn't seem real that I just happened to wake up and a camcorder was there in front of me. It scared me so much because I could see it was me in the viewfinder, but I didn't remember it. I found my way to the bathroom and looked in the mirror and I had hickeys all over my body but the one that stood out most was one that was huge and it was in-between my cheek and neck. I was horrified and terrified. All I wanted was to go home and see my family again.

I walked back to the room and everyone was up, talking on the phone. I knew they were talking about me. Rumor had it that the cops were looking for me and they needed to get rid of me quick. They drove me out to the river on 5th Street and told me to get out. They just drove off. I began walking home; I was scared and I was still trying to piece everything together.

I was less than five minutes from home when my mom came out and saw me. She slapped me across my face. I wasn't at my house for more than a few minutes before they called the police to have me arrested. I couldn't understand what was happening. I tried to speak to the officer in the car but he told me to be quiet.

When I arrived at juvenile detention center and during booking, I broke down and started telling the female officer what I could remember from the night before. She broke down and started crying with me. She said things would be ok and put me in a waiting room while she contacted my parents. I thought everything was going to be alright but a couple moments later I heard her come and tell the other officers that I had told her that I was raped but my family said not to believe me. My hope was lost after that. She strip searched me and finished booking me in. I didn't sleep that night.

My family picked me up about mid-day the next day. No one would talk to me. My mom put me to work making me clean everything, scrub the floors, clean the bathrooms, and rake the leaves. When night finally came my mom set up a stool in the middle of the room and made me sit on it while she slept. She told me that I was not allowed to sleep, because I made her lose sleep. This continued for about a month.

I went back to school and it seemed as though overnight I went from being cool and popular to being the school slut and whore. I was trash after that. I began to get bullied at school and was beat up on the bus. Everyone spoke of the video and how I did all these things. It became too much for me. I wanted to die. I began cutting my arms and legs.

There was a day I was raking leaves outside and my brother was taunting me as I was working. He said that he had heard about the things I said happened, but that no one believed me. He was embarrassed of me. My sister said that if anyone asked her if she knew me she would say no, and she would deny she was my sister. I ran crying to the bathroom and when I saw myself in the mirror it made me angry. I hated the person that I saw, it wasn't me, it was someone else. On the inside I was the same, but the outside was not me. It was an ugly person, a bad daughter, a stupid person. That person was a slut and a whore and I hated her. I grabbed a razor blade and cut my face until I could not see it anymore because of all the blood.

I went to sleep and the next day I was caught by my counselor at school and arrested again. They saw all my cuts all over my body and sent me to a behavioral health facility in Reno. My parents were angry that I was sent there, and they kept yelling about the cost. They kept me there for three and a half months. I had one visitor the entire time and it was no one from my family, it was my sister's boyfriend.

It's hard thinking of those times now because to this day we still don't talk about it.

After leaving the hospital my parents threw away the medicine the hospital had given me and life just resumed. I had to deal with whatever was happening at school and just do my best to make my parents happy. I didn't feel good enough for them. They were so good to me and worked so hard for me and I had hurt them. I wished I could bring them peace because I know they worried about me, even though they didn't know how to help me. They don't know God, and it grieves me so much.

I lost my childhood, and I knew too many things too soon. I honestly don't know how I ended up wanting to go to church. I grew up knowing very little about God, but I thought if I wasn't good enough for my family then why would God love me or want me in His world? I didn't know He was my Creator and sent His Son to die for me. He just seemed too great for little me who couldn't even say no to my friends.

I am understanding that my story is valuable and that my life matters. I have a church family that loves me, and I am surrounded by people who want my success. God speaks straight to my heart through my pastor every week, and I want my story to bring God glory. My past no longer has a hold on me, and it doesn't define me. My God, my Creator, has made me stronger through it and set my feet on a good path.

Defining Moments In Your Day

Day One

Moment of Truth:

"TO EVERYTHING there is a season, and a time for every matter or purpose under heaven: A time to be born..." Ecclesiastes 3:1-2 (Amplified)

"[It is] the Spirit of God that made me [which has stirred me up], and the breath of the Almighty that gives me life [which inspires me]." Job 33:4 (Amplified)

Moment of Reflection:

What were the circumstances and timing of your birth?

Moment of Clarity:

I have had many friends throughout my life who referred to themselves as "accidents." There are no accidental people on this earth. You may have been made to feel like an accident, an unintended mistake, and just in case no one has told you, let me be the one to affirm this truth in you: You are chosen. You are planned for. The Bible says that He calls you by name. You are His precious daughter. Nothing will ever change that. No harsh words, no lies, and no actions against you will ever change the fact that He created you for a purpose and He has placed destiny in your hands.

"Now listen, daughter, don't miss a word:
forget your country, put your home behind you.
Be here—the king is wild for you.
Since he's your lord, adore him."
Psalm 145:10 (MSG)

"It's in Christ that we find out who we are and what we are living for. Long before we first heard of Christ and got our hopes up, he had his eye on us, had designs on us for glorious living, part of the overall purpose he is working out in everything and everyone." Ephesians 1:11 (MSG)

God has an amazing plan for your life. You have gifts, abilities, personality traits and talents that are not repeated in any other human being but you!

Moment of Decision:

What is something in your life that you believe God can use?

Moment of Silence:

God, you are my creator and I thank you for choosing to create me. Help me to understand how you love me completely. I put my trust in you as my heavenly Father, that your plans for me are good. Help me discover more about you in this process of discovering me. Amen.

Day Two

Moment of Truth:

"Then the LORD God formed a man from the dust of the ground and breathed into his nostrils the breath of life, and the man became a living being." Genesis 2:7 (NIV)

"So don't be surprised when I say, 'You must be born again.' The wind blows wherever it wants. Just as you can hear the wind but can't tell where it comes from or where it is going, so you can't explain how people are born of the Spirit." John 3: 7-8 (MSG)

Moment of Reflection:

What does it mean to be a person of the Spirit?

Moment of Clarity:

The entire trinity was present at creation. God the Father, the Son, and the Holy Spirit. The Hebrew word behind Spirit is *ruach*, it means "air in motion."[8] It is the same word for "breath" and it also means "life." When God spoke, breath came out, and the breath took form, in us. It is from the breath of God that we have our life.

We don't have to walk through life and wonder if God is with us, if He is present with us in every moment. It is His breath within us. The Holy Spirit is the breath of God within us and upon our lives. In fact, God's Word gives us great confidence in reminding us how much the Holy Spirit helps us in our weakness.

> *"Meanwhile, the moment we get tired in the waiting, God's Spirit is right alongside helping us along. If we don't know how or what to pray,*

> *it doesn't matter. He does our praying in and for us, making prayer out of our wordless sighs, our aching groans. He knows us far better than we know ourselves, knows our pregnant condition, and keeps us present before God. That's why we can be so sure that every detail in our lives of love for God is worked into something good."* Romans 8:28 (MSG)

Moment of Decision:

What can you do to practice walking through your daily life with the knowledge and assurance that the breath of God, His Holy Spirit, is within you?

Moment of Silence:

Heavenly Father, Thank you for breathing your life into me. Thank you for giving my life value and meaning. I pray that today I will walk with more confidence and face challenges with renewed vitality knowing that you are with me.

Day Three

Moment of Truth:

"If you persist in staying silent at a time like this, help and deliverance will arrive for the Jews from someplace else; but you and your family will be wiped out. Who knows? Maybe you were made queen for just such a time as this." Esther 4:14 (MSG)

Moment of Reflection:

Has there been a time in your life that you could say, "Yes, I was fulfilling my purpose in that situation or moment in time"?

Moment of Clarity:

I think there are moments in all of our lives when we know what God wants us to do, and in spite of all the reasons we come up with for not doing it, for all the good excuses, we know we have missed an opportunity. We can do a lot of good things with our time. Sometimes setting boundaries and keeping priorities is the hardest thing to do.

There are many good causes we can pour our lives into. How do we know the difference between a good cause and a God-cause? I think a God-cause is what you are personally called of God to do. It's different for each and every one of us. Our God is that big and that diverse, and He gives us freedom to be who we are, touching the people in our own circle of influence. He does not put us in a box. He does, however, show us what love looks like, by displaying it for us.

> *"Don't waste your time on useless work, mere busywork, the barren pursuits of darkness. Expose these things for the sham they are. It's a scandal when people waste their lives on things they must do in the darkness where no one will see. Rip the cover off those frauds and see how attractive they look in the light of Christ. Wake up from your sleep, Climb out of your coffins; Christ will show you the light! So watch your step. Use your head. Make the most of every chance you get. These are desperate times!"* Ephesians 5:11-16 (MSG)

There's a great book by Brian Houston, Pastor of Hillsong, called *For This Cause*.[9] In it, he states, "Jesus Christ knew who He was and what the purpose of His life was." He also knew He was here to die. His whole life was summed up in one powerful statement. In John 18:37 Jesus declared,

"For this cause I was born, and for this cause I have come into the world." (NIV)

Without knowing your God cause, it is possible to be pulled in so many directions and have your resources so scattered that you feel like you make little difference to anyone.

But I do know this: You and I were put on this earth to make a difference! You were not an accident, and the people God has placed in your life are there for a reason.

Moment of Decision:

How can you put your priorities into better order to reflect your God-cause this week? Is there anything you could let go of? Is there anything you should add?

Moment of Silence:

Jesus, thank you for making me your priority when you were on earth. You never lost sight of your purpose or your love for me. Help me to begin to understand my purpose as well. Help me keep my eyes on the goal and to make it count. I want my choices and priorities to reflect my love for you.

Day Four

Moment of Truth:

"Whatever you do, work heartily, as for the Lord and not for men," Colossians 3:23 (ESV)

Moment of Reflection:

Do you ever struggle with feelings of guilt over time that you've wasted in your life?

Moment of Clarity:

One of my favorite things about knowing Jesus is this: in spite of all my failures and all my missteps in life, I may have wasted opportunities or wasted time, but God NEVER EVER wastes anything! Every experience that we have had - good, bad, ugly, hurtful, beautiful, helpful, all of it – can be used by God. We sometimes want to hide our past, but God wants to put it to work to help others! It's almost incomprehensible for us to reconcile the idea that instead of hiding our dirty char-stained past, He wants us to hold it out to Him and let Him chisel it and polish it until it becomes something of rare beauty that can truly touch the world around us.

According to legend, when a young boy asked the great Renaissance artist Michelangelo why he was working so hard hitting the block of marble that would eventually become his greatest sculpture, *David*, the artist replied, "Young man, there is an angel inside this rock, and I am setting him free."

You may feel like you have failed God a million times. You make think you've wasted your life on things that don't matter. But nothing is wasted with God as our Master. He is creating a beautiful work of art out of your life!

> *"There has never been the slightest doubt in my mind that the God who started this great work in you would keep at it and bring it to a flourishing finish on the very day Christ Jesus appears."* Philippians 1:6 (MSG)

> *"'For I know the plans I have for you,' declares the LORD, 'plans to prosper you and not to harm you, plans to give you hope and a future.'"* Jeremiah 29:11 (NIV)

> *"So now there is no condemnation for those who belong to Christ Jesus."* Romans 8:1 (NLV)

Moment of Decision:

Knowing that you are forgiven by God, will you look at yourself in the mirror and offer forgiveness to the woman looking back at you? You are loved and treasured and made perfect in Him!

Moment of Silence:

Pray this prayer: Jesus, thank you for redeeming my life, and for redeeming my past. Lord, show me how to offer it up to you to be used for your glory. Help me to make today count. Amen.

Day Five

Moment of Truth:

"Christ arrives right on time to make this happen. He didn't, and doesn't, wait for us to get ready. He presented himself for this sacrificial death when we were far too weak and rebellious to do anything to get ourselves ready. And even if we hadn't been so weak, we wouldn't have known what to do anyway. We can understand someone dying for a person worth dying for, and we can understand how someone good and noble could inspire us to selfless sacrifice. But God put his love on the line for us by offering his Son in sacrificial death while we were of no use whatever to him." Romans 5:8 (MSG)

Moment of Reflection:

Have you accepted Jesus Christ as your Savior? If so, when did it happen? (Did that moment shift your perspective of your life?)

Moment of Clarity:

It is so amazing to comprehend that while we were still sinners, not even thinking of our need of a Savior, Jesus offered Himself up for us! US! Undeserving, unlovely, unknowing, us. Jesus is our redeemer and our friend.

> *"I no longer call you slaves, because a master doesn't confide in his slaves. Now you are my friends, since I have told you everything the Father told me."*
> John 15:15 (NLT)

Jesus not only becomes our friend, His word tells us that He makes all things new. Our life doesn't have to be a repeated pattern of mistakes or a boring rut we settle in to.

> *"This means that anyone who belongs to Christ has become a new person. The old life is gone; a new life has begun!"* 2 Corinthians 5:17 NLT

Moment of Decision:

If you haven't yet accepted Jesus, will you do it now? And if you have, will you renew your commitment to Jesus to make Him the true ruler of your life right now?

Moment of Silence:

Jesus, I realize that I cannot do life on my own. No matter how hard I try, I don't have enough wisdom or strength to live a truly successful life without you. I ask you to fully take up residence in my heart and life today. May I be different from this day forward. Lord, I pray that you will set my feet on a straight path and lead me forward into greater things that you have planned for me. Amen.

Chapter 2
Made For Making History

I STOOD ON the floor on the side of the stage feeling nauseated, sweating, my throat parched and scratchy. The rap artist was pumping up the crowd, the music was loud, hundreds of women were clapping and cheering.

Our Time women were excitedly gathered for our very first conference in February, 2009.

We were there to celebrate the freedom that we have in Jesus. Freedom to be loosed of chains that bound us in the past, freedom to become whatever God was placing in our hearts to be.

I was feeling anything but free. I knew at any moment he would be finished, the crowd would be waiting for the next "wow" moment, and I had to energetically propel myself to center stage to welcome these precious, open-hearted women to their future. But how? I kept thinking, "Who do I think am I? I am a nobody." I felt as if I might hyperventilate, and I wanted to run for the door. "What am I doing? Why did I do this? Why did I put this thing together? I am not made for this!"

My feet felt like they were bolted to the floor, my legs felt like overcooked fettucini. Was my microphone turned on? Would I trip over the cords? Would I remember what I was supposed to say? Would I remember to breathe? To smile? To genuinely express love to these ladies? I so wanted out of there. My mind was racing, while my eyes were searching for ways of escape. It was the longest moment of my life, and I wanted to be anywhere but there.

A Connected Strand

Maybe you've felt that way at times in your own experience. Learning to adapt, adjust, and overcome is something we all strive for, but once in awhile we are called upon to step forward. We feel a sudden shift in the atmosphere and we realize this is our moment. At a time like that, we may feel very alone, like we are the only ones who have ever been there. But the truth is, there have been many before us, and hopefully the legacy we leave behind will hold out such hope and promise that many more will follow behind us.

We are all connected.

We stand upon the shoulders of those who have gone before

us. We must never forget that the time we live in is not separate or solitary. This moment is a connected strand that is woven together in the tapestry of time. No piece is insignificant. No thread is untouched. We are not only connected to one another, but our past is woven into our future.

Knowing where we come from has great power. Quite often, the past can hold such power over us that we become paralyzed, which causes us to live a barren life as a result. The knowledge of our past can empower us to live more fruitful lives filled with hope and tremendous confidence. My desire is to open a window for you. A glimpse backward in time, that will help fuel your passions for your future.

God Loves Women Too

A friend of mine sent me a blog not long ago that asked the question, "God Loves Women Too, Right?"[1] It wasn't the blog itself that bothered me, it was the comments added to it by the readers. One reader said, "All I have heard is how bad women are and we are basically the reason why men are not in the place that God told them to be" and another had been told, "Women belong barefoot in the kitchen."

I just couldn't believe that these discussions were still taking place in America in 2012!

There is so much more at stake upon the earth than petty arguments that relegate women to the background of society. If the enemy can silence our potential and sideline our destiny, he wins!

On July 5, 1995, Hillary Clinton made a speech to the U.N. 4th World Conference on Women. In it she said, "... Women comprise more than half the world's population, 70% of the world's poor, and two-thirds of those who are not taught to read and write. We are the primary caretakers for most of the world's children and elderly. Yet much of the work we do is not valued -- not by economists, not by historians, not by popular culture, not by government leaders...

Tragically, women are most often the ones whose human rights are violated. Even now, in the late 20th century, the rape of women continues to be an instrument of armed conflict. Women and children make up a large majority of the world's refugees. And when women are excluded from the political process, they become even more vulnerable to abuse. I believe now, on the eve of the new millennium, it is time to break the silence... These abuses have continued because, for too long, the history of women has been a history of silence..."[2]

Speak Up

I am so glad that women are beginning to rise up and speak for those who have no voice all across the globe. Human trafficking, marginalization, poverty and abuse should not be tolerated.

Scripture exhorts us to take up their plight. *"Speak up for those who cannot speak for themselves; ensure justice for those being crushed."* Proverbs 31:8 (NLT)

This is not a book about social justice, but it is a call to rise to our potential, and that will look different to each one of us. We live in a free society in America and we have more rights than women in most parts in the world. We have a role to play, right where God has put us.

Inequality is not something that only happens in third-world countries, and it doesn't only exist in the ungodly. Traditionally, inequality exists within the confines of religious society as well. In cities and towns all across America in many mainline denominations, women are not allowed to stand behind a pulpit, not allowed to teach, or lead or have any authority or voice within the church. The Catholic church is a perfect example of the exclusion of women from the highest positions of leadership and authority, as there are no women priests.

While it is true that the Church was God's idea, human beings bring their own imperfect ideas and baggage into the equation. Because some women have been excluded and wounded in the church, they have the idea that God somehow thinks less of women, so they reject Him and the church altogether.

No matter what you have experienced in the past, let me assure you today that God thinks you are amazing! He thinks you are awesome! He thinks you are capable, beautiful, intelligent, worthy and that you have something to say!

The Dreams in Your Heart Are From God

My daughter Alyssa had an interesting encounter at a Christian university this year. Many students in a class were having ongoing discussions about human rights, gender, race and other discrimination issues and one girl in the class actually spoke out and said, "If you have a dream of becoming a leader or a pastor, you might as well put it out of your mind because it's not going to happen." That was her experience talking. My daughter, who grew up being told that she could accomplish anything God put in her heart to accomplish, was completely stunned that this mindset existed in 2012.

In our church, we have female pastors, leaders, teachers, and board members who serve alongside our men. We are blessed to have a lead pastor who doesn't just tolerate women but encourages them to boldly step into positions of leadership. Sadly, it is not like that everywhere.

Have you been faced with these same kinds of opinions? These are the kinds of beliefs that put doubt in your mind and cause you to want to shut up and give up on your God given passions. These opinions are based on lies. When we are faced with opportunities, we will always see opposition. We must learn to refute lies with truth. The dreams that are in your heart are God breathed! The truth says, *"Now to Him Who, by (in consequence of) the [action of His] power that is at work within us, is able to [carry out His purpose and] do superabundantly, far over and above all that we [dare] ask or think [infinitely beyond our highest prayers, desires, thoughts, hopes, or dreams]"* Ephesians 3:20 (AMP)

There is nothing the devil would like more than to silence another entire generation of people who could potentially turn this world upside down for the glory of God. God did not intend for us to sit silently enduring the choices of others with no decision or voice of our own. The Bible is filled with scriptures that remind us of the importance of testimony. Our testimony, our voice, and our story can shift the atmosphere around us, and it can set others free. We need to come to the point where we are absolutely unwilling to sit silent any longer.

If we do not align our thoughts and opinions with the word of God, we will never believe or live in the freedom of the truth. God's intention is that women and men achieve whatever they dream of! Our dreams are from God and they are placed within us for a purpose greater than ourselves.

That One Time it Wasn't Good

Do you realize that in the creation story, after God created each amazing segment of the earth, the Bible says, "He saw that it was good," except one time? You can read the entire creation account in Genesis 1 and 2, but for the sake of our study, let's just look at some of the highlighted events.

> *"In the beginning God created the heavens and the earth..."* (Genesis 1:1)

> *"And God said, 'Let there be light,' and there was light. God saw that the light was **good**, and he separated the light from the darkness."* (Verses 3-4)

> *"God called the dry ground 'land,' and the gathered waters he called 'seas.' And God saw that it was **good**."* (Verse 10)

> *"The land produced vegetation: plants bearing seed according to their kinds and trees bearing fruit with seed in it according to their kinds. And God saw that it was **good**."* (Verse 12)

> *"He also made the stars. God set them in the vault of the sky to give light on the earth, to govern the day and the night, and to separate light from darkness. And God saw that it was **good**."* (Verses 16-17)

> *"So God created the great creatures of the sea and every living thing with which the water teems and that moves about in it, according to their kinds, and every winged bird according to its kind. And God saw that it was **good**."* (Verse 21)

> *"God made the wild animals according to their kinds, the livestock according to their kinds, and all the creatures that move along the ground*

*according to their kinds. And God saw that it was **good**."* (Verse 25)

*"And to all the beasts of the earth and all the birds in the sky and all the creatures that move along the ground—everything that has the breath of life in it—I give every green plant for food. And it was so. God saw all that he had made, and it was **very good**."* (Verse 30-31)

"Then the Lord God formed a man from the dust of the ground and breathed into his nostrils the breath of life, and the man became a living being. Now the Lord God had planted a garden in the east, in Eden; and there he put the man he had formed." (Genesis 2:7-8)

*"The Lord God said, 'It is **not good** for the man to be alone. I will make a helper suitable for him.'"* (Verse 18)

"But for Adam no suitable helper was found. So the Lord God caused the man to fall into a deep sleep; and while he was sleeping, he took one of the man's ribs and then closed up the place with flesh. Then the Lord God made a woman from the rib he had taken out of the man, and he brought her to the man." (Verses 20-22) (NIV)

God set us up to be partners with men, not to be subservient to them. He created us out of Adam's side, not his foot! If you have believed anything other than that, it is not the truth.

The Bible is our standard for truth. In John 8:32 it says,

"Then you will know the truth, and the truth will set you free." If we fully understood what the Word of God reveals about His heart toward us, many of our sisters would not be in such bondage.

It was human beings that thwarted God's perfect plan. You need to know that God loves you, He has purposed you, and He has planned you with His destiny imbedded in your DNA.

Jesus and Women

Jesus came to set the captives free, in every way. We can look at the example He set of how men and women should both serve to advance the Kingdom. He saw the problem even though gender equality was not the cause for which He died. He constantly modeled for men how valued and valuable women were. Let's look at a few examples:

His mother.

God could have provided the Messiah by any means but He chose a woman named Mary in Matthew 1:18. Lowly, humble, and misunderstood, she became the mother of the Messiah!

His friends.

We can look at the example of Mary and Martha. Jesus went to their home many times and ministered there, as well as finding rest with them and their brother Lazarus. We see His example even when Lazarus died in the story found in John 11. Jesus stopped what he was doing and identified with the women and wept with them. He was not aloof and separate. He was their friend.

His ministry.

Jesus chose to treat and minister to men and women equally. He talked to women when it was socially unacceptable to do so. He offered living water and new life to the woman at the well in John 4. We see His example in the woman caught in adultery in John 8. With His persuasive words, Jesus convicted the crowd that would have stoned her. He publicly set her free when others condemned her to death. He liberated them and He liberates us still.

His resurrection.

Matthew 28 reveals that the women were the first at the tomb, the first to see and talk to the angels, and the first to see and talk to HIM in His resurrected form! Wow! I love that. He does not turn away the eager or the bold. He reveals Himself!

As we move further into the New Testament, we see this:

> *"There is neither Jew nor Gentile, neither slave nor free, nor is there male and female, for you are all one in Christ Jesus. If you belong to Christ, then you are Abraham's seed, and heirs according to the promise."* Galatians 3:28-29 (NIV)

All through the New Testament we see women working alongside the men in ministry.

In Acts 8:12, the passage states that men and women were baptized. In Romans 16:1-2, women were made deaconesses. In Acts 16, Phoebe and Lydia both served as single women. Women are acknowledged as faithful servants of the Lord in 2 Timothy 3:14-15, in Hebrews 11:31-38, and in Philippians 4:2-3.

History Makers and World Changers[3]

American history is loaded with examples of women who have been bold enough to seek Him, to experience Jesus being revealed to them and be put into action for the Kingdom. You see, we are a part of a beautiful story that runs throughout time, illustrating that women are not merely spectators in the grand epic, we are at times the main characters, bringing the love of God to the world.

We are not the first ones to realize we are *made for this moment.* We come from a long line of pioneers and history makers. Let me introduce some of them to you.

Edith Mae (Patterson) Pennington. (1902-1974) At one point, Edith was voted Most Beautiful Girl in the United States. She became famous overnight. She became an actress in movies in Hollywood for a time, but as she read her Bible, she realized she wanted something more. The book, *Assemblies of God History, Missions, and Governance* states, "Finally, she exchanged the glamour of Hollywood for the glory of the cross in a Pentecostal church in Oklahoma City." Her husband/business manager didn't approve of the sudden turn around and he left her. Edith's decision to leave Hollywood made news across the country. As reporters gathered to tell her story highlighting her meetings, she morphed from actress to evangelist and pastor.

Anna B. Lock. (1890-1952) Anna was an alcoholic since age 14. She was trapped in a life of sin and drugs, nearly dying many times of overdoses, having nowhere else to turn. She knew that Jesus died on the cross, but she didn't know how to get saved. In 1931 Anna was invited to a revival where a woman preacher hugged her and told her, "Jesus loves you. Jesus needs you." Two years later Anna started her own church, traveled and preached all over North America where many were saved and baptized.

Aimee Semple Mc Pherson. Aimee held Assemblies of God credentials as early as 1919. She rejected the cultural norms that historically limited women, and she built Angeles Temple in Los Angeles. She fed the hungry, clothed the needy, and evangelized the city by using popular culture to attract the masses.

Hattie Hammond. Hattie was the most famous mentor in Pentecost. She was ordained at the age of age 20. Her ministry, Deeper Life Conventions, took her all over North America and she remained a minister for 67 years.

In 1925, during the early days of Assemblies of God missions, we had 250 missionaries on the foreign field. Even back then, the wives were equal partners with the husbands, and 95 of those missionaries were single women! Isn't that amazing to discover their boldness in 1925? They were world-changing pioneers, and they were made for their moment.

It's in Your Blood

That rich tradition and history making potential runs in your blood! If these groundbreaking women could overcome addiction, stigma, past, hardship, social acceptability, age, gender, language barriers, and opposition, what is our excuse?

Women have never breathed freer air or lived in a more opportunity laden time than we do right now. Has God planted dreams deep in your heart that you have been waiting to act upon? Maybe as you've read these stories, God has brought to your remembrance times that He has nudged you but you have resisted. Maybe you have heard Him whisper, yet you've been too afraid to listen? You need to know: you were made for this moment.

Five Stages of Belief

There are five stages of belief that we all go through in our relationship with God. These five stages were common to the history-making women in the Bible, common to the world-changing women of 80 years ago, and they are common to us today.

1. Hearing
2. Curiosity
3. Seeking
4. Revelation
5. Action

Let's look at the five stages through the story of the Samaritan woman at the well in John Chapter 4. Perhaps you can recognize yourself in one of these stages now.

> *"Eventually he came to the Samaritan village of Sychar, near the field that Jacob gave to his son Joseph. Jacob's well was there; and Jesus, tired from the long walk, sat wearily beside the well about noontime. Soon a Samaritan woman came to draw water, and Jesus said to her, 'Please give me a drink.' He was alone at the time because his disciples had gone into the village to buy some food.*
>
> *The woman was surprised, for Jews refuse to have anything to do with Samaritans.[b] She said to Jesus, 'You are a Jew, and I am a Samaritan woman. Why are you asking me for a drink?'*
>
> *Jesus replied, 'If you only knew the gift God has for you and who you are speaking to, you would ask me, and I would give you living water.'"*
> John 4:5-10 (NLT)

Hearing

She heard Him speak directly to her and she was greatly surprised that He would choose to talk to her. Maybe you too are just hearing Him for the first time. Maybe like her, you are also a little guarded. Perhaps you are confused and a little shocked that He would actually be speaking right to your heart. But He is.

If you have felt unloved, unworthy, or worthless as a woman, let today be the day that begins to change that. Maybe you have been put down or abused because of your sex. I'm so sorry for that. I want you to know God was not in that. But God sees you and He's reaching for you now; if He weren't, you certainly would not be reading the pages of this book. Maybe today is your day to receive healing for damages done to you through the words or actions of others. He is speaking to you.

> *"'But sir, you don't have a rope or a bucket,' she said, 'and this well is very deep. Where would you get this living water? And besides, do you think you're greater than our ancestor Jacob, who gave us this well? How can you offer better water than he and his sons and his animals enjoyed?'"* John 4:11-12 (NLT)

Curiosity

She became curious; she wondered what on earth he meant. Maybe you've heard Him for awhile but now you're beginning to get curious. You've even started asking questions. Could it be that you have heard the truth of Jesus and now you are beginning to see the truth of who you really are? You are precious and dearly loved. You are vital to the cause of

Christ! You're not peripheral! You're not on the sidelines, you're in the game!

> *"Jesus replied, 'Anyone who drinks this water will soon become thirsty again. But those who drink the water I give will never be thirsty again. It becomes a fresh, bubbling spring within them, giving them eternal life.'*
>
> *'Please, sir,' the woman said, 'give me this water! Then I'll never be thirsty again, and I won't have to come here to get water.'"* John 4:13-15 (NLT)

Seeking

She began boldly seeking. She heard Him speak to her in such an uncommon way that it made her wonder if this could even be true, but she wanted more of it. She had a past, but she was totally open to something better. Maybe you're at the point where you are becoming bold enough to seek him, to push through your past, to get more of Jesus.

> *"'Go and get your husband,' Jesus told her.*
>
> *'I don't have a husband,' the woman replied.*
>
> *Jesus said, 'You're right! You don't have a husband— for you have had five husbands, and you aren't even married to the man you're living with now. You certainly spoke the truth!'*
>
> *'Sir,' the woman said, 'you must be a prophet. So tell me, why is it that you Jews insist that Jerusalem is the only place of worship, while we Samaritans claim it is here at Mount Gerizim, where our ancestors worshiped?'*
>
> *Jesus replied, 'Believe me, dear woman, the time is coming when it will no longer matter*

whether you worship the Father on this mountain or in Jerusalem. You Samaritans know very little about the one you worship, while we Jews know all about him, for salvation comes through the Jews. But the time is coming—indeed it's here now— when true worshipers will worship the Father in spirit and in truth. The Father is looking for those who will worship him that way. For God is Spirit, so those who worship him must worship in spirit and in truth.'

The woman said, 'I know the Messiah is coming—the one who is called Christ. When he comes, he will explain everything to us.'

Then Jesus told her, 'I Am the Messiah!'" John 4:16-26 (NLT)

Revelation

The story unfolds like ripples in a stream with undercurrents of His kindness and the promise of life rippling over her feet until this revelation of His identity pours out like a gush of freedom and joy upon her.

Maybe you're at the place where Jesus is revealing himself to you and you are amazed and you stand in awe of the revelation of how much he loves you.

"Just then his disciples came back. They were shocked to find him talking to a woman, but none of them had the nerve to ask, 'What do you want with her?' or 'Why are you talking to her?'

The woman left her water jar beside the well and ran back to the village, telling everyone, 'Come and see a man who told me everything I ever did! Could he possibly be the Messiah?' So the people came streaming from the village to see him." John 4:27-30 (NLT)

Sisters taking action together

Action

She left her water jug and went running. She was excited and beyond happy! She told everyone what had happened. She was moved to action. A revelation of Jesus always produces action in us. Once we know who He is, we suddenly realize who we are! We are His!

Where do you find yourself on this scale of one through five? Maybe you're still not sure you're even on the scale, but friend, let me assure you, you are. This is your time! You were made for this moment! This message of living water and freedom was not just for those women of the past who paved the way, those pioneers of old. This message is for you! You were made to make history too! You are paving the way for someone else to follow right at this time. So rise up, girlfriend, rise up! You have a beautiful foundation under your feet, and you were made for this moment!

Jean's Story
In Her Own Words

I was the oldest of four children. I was just sure that I was an "accident" because I was a honeymoon baby. I was born nine months later on March 13, 1927. I never heard the words "I love you" from my mom and all four of us children grew up very poor and some days we went without food.

When I was thirteen years old, I went away to a youth camp and found Jesus. A few years later I met my future husband at a spring break dance when he cut in on me and my dance parter. Jim lived in San Francisco and was handsome, strong (he served three years in the Marines in active combat) and everything I had dreamed of. Not much later, Jim proposed and I planned and paid for the entire wedding. Because I was not Catholic (my parents claimed to be Baptist), my dad refused to walk me down the aisle in the Catholic church and my mother would not contribute to the wedding. Jim's mom never fully accepted me either because of her religion. I agreed to take six weeks of classes as a part of the Catholic religion to promise to raise my children Catholic. Jim and I were married November 6, 1949 and later had two children.

My mother still remained absent in my life and never really liked her grandchildren. Jim was an inspector with the San Francisco Police Department. He served in the sex crimes and narcotic division and his macho image took priority in his life. He began to drink heavily. He provided for our family but he was absent in his fatherly role.

For twenty-five years I raised and nurtured our family but never returned to church after my encounter at camp when I was thirteen years old. Jim continued to drink and work as a police officer. When I was 44 years old a neighbor gave my son a book to give to me. It was a book titled, *God Can Do It Again* by Katherine Kuhlman. I read the book (a chapter a day because I was so convicted), and I literally ran back to church.

I was convicted, I needed a change, and most of all I needed Jesus. Jim was okay with me going to church because he thought he could continue with his lifestyle of drinking and I would not interfere. But I began to pray for Jim. Everyday I prayed for my husband's salvation. Every time I was in church, I prayed for my husband's salvation. Every person who asked if I needed prayer, I would ask them pray for my husband's salvation. I prayed for four years.

On July 30, 1975 Jim woke up hung over and desperate. I wrote out the sinner's prayer for Jim, and he closed the bedroom door behind him. I knelt at the door and pleaded with God one last time to save my husband. Jim accepted Jesus that day and was immediately delivered from alcoholism (no withdraws, no drying out). Within six months Jim and his partner, Jim Crowley started Cops for Christ which was the first Christian organization in the 127 years of the SFPD.

Jim became a prayer warrior and saw God perform many miracles and salvations in his time as a Christian. Including when our daughter and her husband came to the Lord. Jim would have prayer meetings in the interrogation room of The Hall of Justice where he prayed for people and witnessed many healings. One of which was a young lady's leg lengthening after she received prayer for her legs to be the same length. He was featured on the 700 Club twice and traveled as a speaker within the Cops for Christ ministry.

My mother never fully accepted Jim and I, even after our salvation. But God did. Jim went home to be with the

Lord after losing his fight with cancer in 1996. God has sustained me and given me joy and comfort every day of my life.

I am now 85 years old, and to this day I believe that a Christian's most powerful resource is communion with God through prayer. James 5:16 says, "The faithful earnest prayer of a righteous man has great power and wonderful results."

Defining Moments In Your Day

Day 1

Moment of Truth:

"'Your name will no longer be Jacob,' the man told him. 'From now on you will be called Israel, because you have fought with God and with men and have won.'" Genesis 32:28 (NIV)

Moment of Reflection:

Have you ever felt as though, because of your gender, you were fighting both God and men?

Moment of Clarity:

As I read the story of Jacob and put this verse into proper context, I understand that Jacob was worried about many things. He was concerned about a confrontation he would have with a man the next day and He was worried that God was holding Him back from entering the promised land, so he was getting alone with God so that he could straighten out all his cares before Him. It is at this point that an angel comes to wrestle with Jacob, both physically and spiritually. Many times throughout our lives it seems that everyone is an enemy, even God. We feel like all we do is fight.

We must try to remember that struggle isn't just for struggle's sake. Sometimes God is trying to get our attention, sometimes He is trying to make us shift gears, and other times He simply wants to change us. Do we trust Him enough to know that He works everything for our good?

Romans 8:28 says, *"And we know that God causes everything to work together[a] for the good of those who love God and are called according to his purpose for them."* (NLT)

God works everything out for our good when we love Him.

> *"But now, O Jacob, listen to the Lord who created you.*
> *O Israel, the one who formed you says,*
> *'Do not be afraid, for I have ransomed you.*
> *I have called you by name; you are mine.'"*
> Isaiah 43:1 (NLT)

The prophet Isaiah reminds us as he recounts this story that Jacob's name had been changed and that what he went through changed him, but he was precious to God. I believe the same is true of you and I. Even though we may be going through a circumstance that may change us, we should not be afraid. When we face challenging situations that make us question our identity, it is as though a steady hand is reaching for us saying "I have called you by name. You belong to me!"

Moment of Decision:

Will you make a decision to trust God in the battles you are facing?

Moment of Silence:

Dear Jesus, thank you for your word that confirms your love for me. Thank you for calling me by name and reminding me that I am yours. Help me to trust you with this battle I'm in. I want to understand that you will use it to change me for good and I belong to you. Amen.

Day 2

Moment of Truth:

"For if you remain silent at this time, relief and deliverance for the Jews will arise from another place, but you and your father's family will perish. And who knows but that you have come to your royal position for such a time as this?" Esther 4:14 (NIV)

Moment of Reflection:

Have there been times in your life when you have remained silent and you wished you hadn't?

Moment of Clarity:

Many of us grew up in an era of extremely strict parenting when children were to be "seen and not heard." It is against this backdrop that many find messages to speak up, to stand out, to make our point of view understood, to be conflicting. It is difficult to bend the rules of such a strict upbringing.

When Esther became queen, God knew he had her right where he needed her. He knew a generation of Jewish people were soon to be at stake and He needed someone who would stand up for them. He needed someone who would not be silent.

What about where you are? Does God have you right where He needs you? Is there a situation within your sphere of influence that needs your voice? Maybe you should be speaking out against bullying at school, maybe you should be speaking up for those who can't speak for themselves like lobbying our government against abortion, or perhaps you simply need to speak up for yourself. Send your words into the atmosphere to change your situation in life. Saying, "You can not hit me anymore," or "I will not subject myself to those harmful words any longer," or "I will not fill my mind with negativity that drags me down any more." By saying "enough is enough" we give ourselves the courage and permission to change our lives.

Moment of Decision:

If you have been silent about a matter for too long, will you begin speaking out as God gives you wisdom?

Moment of Silence:

God, help me to not remain silent when my voice could make the difference in someone's life, or even in my own. I want all you have for me and that means I need to be free of stifling my thoughts or my voice.

Day 3

Moment of Truth:

"She speaks with wisdom, and faithful instruction is on her tongue." Proverbs 31:26 (NIV)

Moment of Reflection:

When you speak, do you measure the weight of your words?

Moment of Clarity:

Part of having wisdom in knowing when to speak involves speaking to build up and edify others. To edify means to strengthen, instruct, encourage and enlighten. The Bible tells us we are to do this. *"So encourage each other and build each other up, just as you are already doing."* 1 Thessalonians 5:11 (NIV)

In this age of social media, it's funny how people post things to social media sites that they would never have the courage to say to someone's face or to speak out loud. Some people feel as though they are separated from their words because they're out in cyber space. Words, once spoken (or posted), can't be taken back.

Moment of Decision:

Will you use your words to build up and encourage someone today?

Moment of Silence:

Heavenly Father, I pray that you will help me exercise wisdom in the words I speak and communicate to others. I pray that you will begin to open my eyes so I will become more aware of those who need an encouraging word, and help me know just what to say. Thank you for giving me the ability to communicate and help me to use it for you. Amen

Day 4

Moment of Truth:

"'I will do everything you say,' Ruth replied." Ruth 3:5 (NLT)

Moment of Reflection:

Is there an older woman in your life that you would trust enough to do everything she says?

Moment of Clarity:

Ruth and Naomi had built a long relationship together. Ruth was a young woman who married Naomi's son. But Naomi's husband died. Then Naomi's sons (including Ruth's husband) died. It was just Ruth and Naomi getting through life together. Ruth trusted that Naomi had her best interest at heart and she also trusted her wisdom. Ruth respected and loved Naomi very much.

It is not easy to find a close relationship like that, especially if you have no family. We use that as an excuse sometimes for a lack of close bonds with people, but in reality, Naomi and Ruth were not even related.

It takes intentional effort for us to find another woman we really admire and wish to emulate. Once you find one, it takes an investment of time on the parts of both people. But it is worth the effort. There is a wealth of wisdom within those women who have experienced a little more of life than we have. Ask someone to coffee, ask her advice, look for God connections you already may have and let them grow!

Moment of Decision:

Who is someone you will try to build a relationship with?

Moment of Silence:

Jesus, I pray that you will help me to find an older woman who will encourage me and help me grow. Help me to be a blessing to her as well. Amen.

Day 5

Moment of Truth:

"When Naomi saw that Ruth was determined to go with her, she said nothing more." Ruth 1:8 (NLT)

Moment of Reflection:

Is there a younger woman in your life who you could encourage and help pave the way for?

Moment of Clarity:

Naomi had been trying to get Ruth to leave, to go back to her mother and her native land, but Ruth would not leave. Ruth was really a misfit in Naomi's world; she didn't know the rituals or customs of this land, but she experienced something special when she was with Naomi. I believe it was the goodness and kindness of God. So Naomi stopped arguing and brought her along.

Have you ever had a younger girl in your life that just would not leave? God has a way of attaching people to us that need what we have. We have experience. We have knowledge. We have food. We have love. We have Jesus. Young women who lack those things at home often connect to those things in me.

Is it a hassle? Sometimes. Is it inconvenient? Usually. Is it worth it? Always.

Moment of Decision:

Who is the younger woman in your life who you can bring along?

Moment of Silence:

Dear Lord, Help me to remember how patient and loving you have been with me so that I can share my life with others in the same way. I pray you will bring more "Ruth's" into my world so I can wrap my arms around them and bring them along. Amen.

Chapter 3
Made For Ownership

MY HUSBAND and I waited nearly eight years before we had children and from my husband's viewpoint there was always another goal to be accomplished: a Master's Degree to be completed, or occupational experience to be gained, or a Doctoral Degree to be earned. From my perspective, I was growing tired of always waiting. Life was on hold. So once he finally relented and agreed that it was time for us to start a family, I wanted to make up for lost time and give him no opportunity to change his mind. We had three kids in three years. I'm sure people questioned my sanity at times.

My husband then took a commission with the US Navy serving the Marine Corps in 29 Palms, California as a chaplain when our youngest son was born. My husband flew to the East Coast for training while I sold our home in Washington, packed up the household goods, and met him on the way to California. It was a crazy time in my life, and I just dug down deep and got through every day the best I could.

I remember my pediatrician saying, "Well Mrs. Friend, don't try to accomplish too much, and don't strive for perfection. Basically at this stage of your life, it's just suicide prevention - you just want them to make it through alive." I was determined to have a better experience than that! I had waited so long!

Once we arrived in 29 Palms, I immediately started learning what being an officer's wife entailed, as well as learning the duties of a chaplain's wife in caring for the spiritual well being of hundreds of wives who looked up to me for an example in the stressful times of deployments and transfers.

I remember distinctly a time when an older officer's wife came to me and asked me to become the leader of Protestant Women of the Chapel. I said a very terse "No," thinking to myself, "Not on your life!"

I thought of all the reasons why I couldn't do it, but none of the reasons were the things I just mentioned. I said "no" because I was terrified! I had never led *anything* before, I had never been very involved in Women's Ministries, and I had never even taught a Bible study before. I thought I was not at all qualified, not a leader, and not cut out for that kind of job. No. No. No.

I had a lot of external reasons I could have blamed for my unavailability, but if I would have been honest, all those reasons were just a smokescreen. The real excuses were internal. In my innermost being, I knew I was unworthy to be in that position. Maybe you can relate to those feelings. Busyness is the easiest card to play when we need an excuse, but it's not the real reason we shy away from His calling.

The Cards You're Dealt

We are all so busy. Our hands are so full. We are taught from an early age to "play the hand you're dealt." There are so many cards! We are daughter, sister, wife, mother, coach, encourager, friend, disciplinarian, cook, maid, financial planner, investigator, and the list goes on and on and on.

Your cards may look different from mine, but you certainly have a lot of them. We hold them in our hands and play them as wisely as we can, but how are we supposed to know when to reach across the table for another card? Will it be any good? Will we be able to play it well?

Women have a knack for adaptation. We do what we have to do. We have skill in multi-tasking. We see a need and fill it. We keep the world turning properly on it's axis for those we love.

But when things quiet down and every immediate cry is silenced, we catch our breath, and we begin to hear the whisper. We start to consider, "Hey, what about me?" You know that voice. The nudge from deep within that says, "You were born for something more."

As quickly as we hear the question, we are flooded with all the reasons why we shouldn't be asking such a question.

I have friends who were told from an early age, "You won't amount to anything. You're just a stupid girl." Those of us who escaped those kinds of accusations as children were lucky. It's a shame that so much of our adult self-esteem is garnered on the elementary school playground and from careless adults who attack the value of our worth before we are even old enough to prove otherwise.

If we don't hear these things from others, sometimes we hear them inside our own heads. Voices like this, "Shhh... Be quiet. Don't step up. Don't stand out. Someone will surely find you out and tell the truth about who you really are. You will be put in your place for sure!"

Two Choices

From the beginning of recorded time in the Garden of Eden until now, doubts and lies have been Satan's chief weapons of choice to keep us down. He wields his weapons with skill and expertise. He uses our weakest points and our greatest fears to expose insecurities. He tells us his well constructed lies. His goal is to keep us from God's intended purpose for our lives.

Maybe you've heard some of his lies: "You're not smart enough. You're not pretty enough. You didn't come from the right background. You're not worthy. You're not qualified. Who are you trying to fool?"

When these kinds of thoughts enter our mind, we have one of two choices to make. The first choice is this: We can set up residence in these thoughts and let them ruminate in our mind. If we do this, we will immediately recall every past mistake and personal failure we have experienced and align ourselves with them until they back up the claims that we are not good enough.

Our second choice is to get ourselves aligned with the truth of God's word and what He says about us. (We talked about what God says about us in Chapter One. If you have forgotten already, let me encourage you to go back and read them again.)

God's word tells us who we really are! When we get a glimpse of Jesus' heart for us as we reflect upon God's word, it has the potential to change everything! All of a sudden we walk with our head up. We carry ourselves with confidence, knowing that we are important. We are capable. We are valued. And it's not just that we have value to God, but we are absolutely valuable to His kingdom.

It is revolutionary when we grasp the fact that we are placed on this earth for a reason, and it is within the realm of possibility, in fact it's absolutely doable, for us to make an impact in our world. Not only is it doable, it is expected! We were made to take ownership of our lives.

Abbey Road

When I visited London recently, one of the things I wanted to see was Abbey Road, where the Beatles recorded their final album. It was my first morning in London, and it seemed like a simple thing to find. Abbey Road is a famous landmark, right? But when you go to an unfamiliar place, you simply cannot anticipate how big it will be or how spread apart places are or even how much it will cost you to get where you want to go. I looked in the travel books, I looked on the maps, and it looked way out on the edge of town, far from the downtown area. It looked like a tiny speck in such an expansive city. I began to think there was no way I was going to get to see it.

I asked the concierge in the lobby of my hotel to show me where I was on the map. He circled the spot where I was. I thought it looked pretty close to Abbey Road.

I stood in the lobby. I looked out across the street to an Islamic Center and down the street, and I saw lots of little Middle Eastern shops. My roommate was asleep. I was all alone. I didn't know the area. It was raining. I thought I could get lost, or I could get mugged. I could take too long. I could get soaking wet. All very good excuses to go back to my room.

But I didn't want excuses to stop me after I had come such a long distance. I really wanted to see this place I had always heard about. So off I trotted. (As they say in the UK.) GPS in hand, I discovered it really wasn't that hard to navigate. I took a couple turns down little tree lined streets, and I soon found myself turning onto Abbey Road. I took some snapshots of myself and kept walking in the blowing rain until I was standing right in front of the studio. I did it! I saw the painted stripes on the road where John, Paul,

Ringo and George had that iconic picture taken. I made it to my goal and saw Abbey Road with my own eyes!

But just a short time earlier, I had believed my own deception that it was just too far. Once I got past the idea that that might not be true, once I got the map and realized that it may have been closer than I thought, I was still bombarded with innumerable excuses.

It's no different for us when we are finding out who we are in Christ. We get past the lies we've been told, we get past the initial understanding of God's love for us, and then we are faced with all these excuses for not moving any further forward.

Excuses We Give and Lies We Believe

You may have heard God's voice speaking to you. You may have been asked to do something you don't think you're capable of doing. You may have been pushed into doing something way beyond your comfort zone. When you find yourself in that place, it becomes the easiest thing in the world to make up excuses, the hand of cards you've been dealt is full of them.

My past is not good enough.

I have a friend who confided in me, "I didn't think God could forgive me, let alone love me. I'm embarrassed of who I used to be, and if anyone knew, they would not want to be around me so I keep to myself." For years she let this excuse keep her from doing anything to help anyone else. She lived within the safety of the cocoon she had built, but that cocoon also kept her isolated.

God created us to live in community and to reach out to one another. An ugly past is not enough of an excuse to hold you back. By the way, no one has a perfect past. "Perfect" doesn't exist outside of heaven. God wants to use us in all our imperfections. When we think we are broken beyond repair, He shines His beauty through all our cracks and flaws and creates a masterpiece in us.

I'm afraid.

Katherine Hepburn holds the record for the most Best Actress Oscar wins. She has won Emmys and Tonys and Golden Globes. She is known far and wide as one of the greatest female stars of all time. Her very first leading role was in a production of *The Big Pond*. She got the role when the producer dismissed the original actress at the last moment and substituted Hepburn. She was terror stricken. Hepburn arrived late and stumbled over her lines, tripped over her feet, and spoke so quickly she was almost incomprehensible. She was also dismissed from the film, but she continued to understudy and gain small stock company roles. One article stated that, "She was officially labeled 'box office poison' in 1938."[1]

If Katherine had stopped acting because she was afraid or because of her failure, she would have never become the success that we know her to have been. Fear will keep you from your destiny if you don't take action to overcome it.

One thing you can do to overcome fear is to tell your story. Your life - your story - is yours and yours alone. No one else can tell it like you can. When we let our story and the experiences we've had be expressed to others, we feel the confidence and power that is released because we know what God has brought us through and what He has taught us. Nothing can ever take those things away from us. They're like gold in our vault. Don't hoard it. Own your story and use it for God's glory.

I'm insignificant.

We have a penchant for self talk that is dangerous to our futures when we say, "I am a nobody. I'm not from a famous or well-known family. I don't even know anyone famous."

God has a way of using the people that no one else notices. He is quite good at using those who are willing, not those who the world thinks are important. Look at how God chose the mother of the Messiah. When the angel appeared to Mary, she was so stunned that she asked how this could be. In her song of praise to the Lord, it is recorded that she knew she was a nobody who became a somebody in one encounter with the Almighty God.

> *"Mary responded, Oh, how my soul praises the*
> *Lord. How my spirit rejoices in God my Savior!*
> *For He took notice of his lowly servant girl, and*
> *from now on all generations will call me blessed."*
> Luke 1:46-47 (NLT)

If He can look down upon a lowly peasant girl and do something so amazing, what makes us think He can't do something wonderful with and through us?

I'm not qualified.

It's completely probable that we feel unqualified, unprepared, and ill-equipped to fill the role that God is calling us to fill. Those feelings are difficult to overlook, but they can be overcome. There is training available for anything. Much of it is free through the internet. We can practically become experts in anything if we put enough time in. In Malcolm Gladwell's book, *Outliers*[2], he claims that all it takes is 10,000 hours spent in any one hobby or field to make you an expert in it. We can take classes. We can ask questions. We can read books. Getting qualified will cost us something, but staying unqualified will cost us so much more.

God is more concerned with our obedience and willingness than He is with our current abilities. I love how Bill Johnson stated it once, he suggested that when you're willing to do what you're unqualified to do, that's what qualifies you. Our willingness is the first and most important ingredient in the process.

A familiar saying in my circle is this: God doesn't call the qualified, He qualifies the called.

I'm too old.

One thing I love about God is that He is the God of second chances. And third. And fourth. And fifth... You may think you've missed your chance. You may have just flat out given up on your dreams and let them die. But let me assure you, they are not dead, and it's not too late.

I once read a great article about late bloomers, in it the author said, "In most fields, age really does not matter. In fact, it can become one of the most valuable assets you have, as experience often counts more than unschooled talent." [1] There are many examples in that same article[3] of people who found success later in life. Here are a few:

F. Murray Abraham got his first decent screen role as an actor when he was 45 years old. The role was in the movie *Amadeus* for which he won an Academy Award for his dazzling portrayal of Antonio Salieri. He had thought of giving up acting just two years prior but didn't.

Andrea Bocelli didn't start singing opera seriously until the age of 34 years old. Some 'experts' told him it was simply too late to begin.

Stan Lee, creator of *Spider-Man*, was 43 years old when he began drawing his legendary superheroes. His partner Jack Kirby was 44 years old when he created *The Fantastic Four*.

Julia Child didn't even learn to cook until she was almost 40 years old and didn't launch her popular show until she was 50.

Harlan Sanders, the Colonel Sanders of Kentucky Fried Chicken fame, was 66 years old when he began to promote his savory style of southern cooking and create his empire.

Laura Ingalls Wilder began writing as a columnist in her 40s. Contrary to a belief begun by the TV series about her family, the popular *Little House* books were not written when she was a young girl at all. They were written and published when the 'girl' was in her sixties!

George Eliot once wrote, "It is never too late to become what you might have been."

I honestly don't understand where the concept came from that suggests we can simply retire our Christianity when we get to a certain age. With God as our help, there is always a new hill to climb and a new chapter to write. As long as we are breathing, there is something for us to do for His Kingdom.

The Bible declares, *"But the godly will flourish like palm trees and grow strong like the cedars of Lebanon. For they are transplanted to the Lord's own house. They flourish in the courts of our God. Even in old age they will still produce fruit; they will remain vital and green."* Psalms 92:12-14 (NLT)

If you need some more evidence of aging history makers, here is proof of life after wrinkles:

Moses and Aaron were eighty and eighty-three and they were still challenging people forward.

Joshua and Caleb were past their eighties when they were leading their people to victory.

Daniel was over eighty at the time he was used by God when he was thrown in the Lions Den and when he was dreaming dreams. Zachariah and Elizabeth were both "getting on in years" when God worked through them to deliver John the Baptist into the world. Paul was writing, traveling, and leading even when he was well advanced in years.

As a child of God, a daughter of the King, there is no such thing as being too old or beginning too late. God is never early, and He is never late. He is always right on time. If you still have breath left in you, there is a reason for it. He is not finished with you, so buck up and move ahead, gorgeous girl. You may not do everything you wish you could do, but you can do something! This is our life! Let's own it!

A Word About Seasons

There is wisdom in knowing that we go through seasons in life and that situation that is currently happening in your life will not be a constant in your life. Sometimes we have responsibilities to others that must come first, and our own dreams must be put on hold for a time. When God says "Wait," it doesn't mean it's forever, and it doesn't mean that He's saying, "No."

If God has given you small children to care for, or children with disabilities, or aging parents, they are your calling in that season. You don't need to feel guilty for not "saving the world." For right now, they are your world and by caring for them, you are saving the world.

No task is insignificant, and no calling is less than another. God has placed you where you are, in the season you are in, and you must embrace it and take responsibility for it.

It may be difficult, but God has equipped you for it. Before we can ever expect more from God, we have to do the best with what's in our hand. God sees and honors faithfulness.

These difficult seasons are often a testing ground, and they reveal our heart. When Jonah had been running from what God had called him to do, he ended up in the belly of the whale. Before the answer came, before he was saved, before God's miracles came, he began thanking God for His miraculous saving grace - it had taken the belly of the whale to finally come to terms with God and what He was requiring of Jonah in this season of His life. In Jonah 2:9 Jonah's prayer is recorded,

> *"But I, with shouts of grateful praise,*
> *will sacrifice to you.*
> *What I have vowed I will make good.*
> *I will say, 'Salvation comes from the Lord.'"* (NIV)

In seasons of difficulty, in seasons that require years of patience, even in times we'd wish to be anywhere else, we should be full of praise and thanksgiving. When we can't see the proof of God's hand, we can still understand the law of the harvest says that something is happening when it looks like nothing is happening. As trees are getting ready to bloom yet we see no buds on the branches, we know there is stuff going on inside the root system long before the evidence reveals itself in leaves or fruit on the outside of the tree.

God is just as interested in the process as He is in the promises being fulfilled in our lives. Sometimes He takes us through a process that feels like nothing but delay, but He is growing us and teaching us things that will make the promised end so much sweeter.

We have opportunities to accept what God is doing in our lives and press in to it or to reject what God is calling us to.

When God's Chosen One Refused

Over a period of time I began to realize that my excuses were not innocent time wasters, they were actually disobedience. I believe that God was calling me long before I ever heard Him, and He persisted even when I resisted. I eventually had to come to terms with the fact that my resistance was turning in to refusal.

If someone had asked me, "Would you ever refuse the Lord?" I would have said, "No! Never!" But if we make enough excuses and waste enough time, our lives pass by and we will find that is exactly what we have done. Refused.

In 1 Samuel, there is a story about refusal that begins with the people of Israel asking for a king of their own. They wanted to be like all the other nations they saw. Having God as their very own personal God and the prophet Samuel on their side to lead them was not enough. They wanted a ruler. So God gave them a man named Saul to be their king.

The prophet tried to warn them that they'd be better off without one, but they wouldn't listen.

> *"But the people refused to listen to Samuel's warning. 'Even so, we still want a king,' they said. 'We want to be like the nations around us. Our king will judge us and lead us into battle.'...Then Samuel took a flask of olive oil and poured it over Saul's head. He kissed Saul and said, "I am doing this because the Lord has appointed you to be the ruler over Israel, his special possession...As Saul turned and started to leave, God gave him a new heart, and all Samuel's signs were fulfilled that day."* 1 Samuel 8:19-20, 10:1,9

So God searched His people and found the right man. He was taller than most, handsome, and righteous. Verse 9 shows us that God provided exactly what Saul needed to complete the task He was being called to. God gave him a new heart to lead.

But just a few verses later, Samuel announces to the people that they have a king, all the people gather, they want to see this new ruler. But no one can find him.

> *"So they asked the Lord, 'Where is he?' And the Lord replied, 'He is hiding among the baggage.'*

> *So they found him and brought him out, and he*
> *stood head and shoulders above anyone else."* 1
> Samuel 10:22

His first act as King was to hide. Fear and insecurity are real, but when God appoints you to a task, you must come to a point where you will quit hiding, and stand.

Over the next three chapters we are given a glimpse of Saul's rule, his military conquests, his victories, his defeats, the times that he listened for God's voice, and the times that he didn't listen. He began to do what was right in his own eyes, and as God kept instructing, kept calling to him, Saul's heart turned cold and he refused to obey the word of the Lord.

In Chapter 13, Saul was given instructions from God, but he did things his own way, this is what happened:

> *"How foolish!" Samuel exclaimed. "You have not*
> *kept the command the Lord your God gave you.*
> *Had you kept it, the Lord would have established*
> *your kingdom over Israel forever. 14 But now your*
> *kingdom must end, for the Lord has sought out a*
> *man after his own heart. The Lord has already*
> *appointed him to be the leader of his people,*
> *because you have not kept the Lord's command."*
> 1 Samuel 13:13 (NIV)

Obedience was expected of King Saul. The nation was dependent on him to do right in the sight of God, to be a good servant of God, and to become a mighty king of God. But he didn't. And he wasn't. God grew tired of the waiting, weary of the disappointment of Saul's excuses, and He finally gave up and chose a new king instead.

We can only ignore the voice of the Lord so long.

Eventually, He may stop whispering to us, or He may choose another. Even when God was calling Esther He reminded her that if she did not speak up and take ownership, He would raise up another, but it wouldn't be in her generation. A whole generation of people would be lost, waiting for someone else to rise up. Do we want that to be the case in our lives?

It scared me to death when I first made that realization; God had a job for me to do, and if I refused to step up, he just might pick someone else! My only response was to say, "No God, don't choose someone else. You chose me! You made me able! You made me uniquely perfect for the task at hand. I will pick myself up and I will complete the task to which you have called me." Ownership is what He asks for.

Another way to explain ownership is as the possession of property. God wants us to possess the land that He has given us. We sometimes have the attitude that the place where we are doesn't really belong to us, and we act like squatters. We sneak around begging as though we are illegal tenants when God has given us full possession of the land already.

When we don't feel able, we must make choices that will bring us closer to being able. When we don't feel qualified, we must get qualified. We are not helpless victims in life. We are overcomers. We are strong and mighty in the Lord.

God knows us better than anyone else. He knows our past, our weakness, our frailty, and He chooses us anyway! He always makes allowances for our imperfections and compensates for our weaknesses. He knows our capabilities and our flaws. He also knows our potential.

God chose us, but we get to choose too. We can choose to hold on to our excuses and miss every opportunity to step into the life God is calling us to, or we can choose obedience. We can live a life of great adventure and discovery if we choose to listen and obey the sound of His voice.

It's not an accident that He has called you. Don't let excuses rob you of your destiny. Only you can do what you do! You were made for this moment!

Sue's Story
In Her Own Words

I grew up in a home where I was never allowed to speak of pain. If we didn't speak of the pain, then it didn't exist, and the image of a wonderful family would always be intact. Actually, there was a lot of pain in our home. There was more pain, more abuse, and more secrets than there was love. Somewhere along the way, in my childhood, I determined that it was my job to rescue my parents and my brothers and sister. No matter how many times I would intervene I couldn't make things right. Mind you, the abuse started when I was eight years old and from that time I had determined that I was a failure. Mostly, I was a failure at helping those that I loved the most. With every failed attempt at helping those closest to me, I viewed myself as a bigger failure. I have lived most of my life trying to change that picture of myself. The most painful fail happened five years ago.

My biggest fail ever was not being able to save my husband's life on the night that he choked to death.

I don't usually go home between work and church events. On this Friday night I felt that I should make the extra stop because I had been out of town, and I wanted to visit with my husband before the evening's event. As it turned out, I never made it to the event. While eating dinner, my husband, Ken, swallowed a bite of food and began to choke. At first I didn't realize what was happening, he walked over to our kitchen sink, and as he bent over the sink, I tried to administer first aid. I tried delivering blows to the back, and that did not work. Then I tried to wrap my arms around him to attempt the Heimlich maneuver, but as he was so much bigger than I, and I couldn't do it effectively. When he passed out, the panic set in. I had never felt so alone and scared. I alternated between crying to Ken and begging him to come out of it, to pounding on his chest, to screaming out to God.

Desperately, I ran to my neighbor's house for help. I banged on her door, crying over and over again to please help me, but she refused to open her door. Running back to the house, I dialed 911 and did all that they instructed me to do. It seemed as if hours had passed by when it was actually minutes. Pain always seems longer than reality. The paramedics did come and they were able to get his heart beating again, but Ken never came out of the coma and he died.

I cannot tell you how huge the word - FAILURE - seemed to me during my mourning. I had failed to save the love of my life. He looked to me for help and I didn't do enough. His eyes cried out for rescue and I didn't. He died. I failed in a big way.

It has taken me some years to even share the pain of that night. And it has taken that long to get past the fail. My head may tell me that it was an accident, but my heart has to heal from the pain.

The truth is that while I wasn't able to save my husband, I was there. He was never alone, and I did everything that I knew to do. While I failed at saving his life, I am not defined as a failure. I am NOT defined as a failure. Even as I type those words, it is a fight to get past what I had allowed to define me. I had allowed my fails to define me until I had to live past the biggest fail of all.

God doesn't see me through my fails; He sees me in spite of my fails. He defines me as a living breathing success and I will choose to see me through His gracious eyes.

Defining Moments In Your Day

DAY 1

Moment of Truth:

"But Moses pleaded with the Lord, "O Lord, I'm not very good with words. I never have been, and I'm not now, even though you have spoken to me. I get tongue-tied, and my words get tangled." Exodus 4:10-14 (NLT)

Moment of Reflection:

Have you ever made excuses when you were asked to do something beyond your comfort zone?

Moment of Clarity:

It's funny how even when we KNOW it is God himself who has spoken to us, we still tell Him all the reasons why we can't do it. It is GOD! The one who created us, formed us, and knows all we are capable of, and we still make excuses. Moses was not alone in this.

When I was very young, I was a stutterer. It was a

terrible affliction for a young person craving self expression. It kept me very anxious and at times silent. My parents tried making me sing my sentences to get through it. I think it left scars on my psyche.

I never wanted to speak in a group. Even in a small group setting, if questions or reading was passed from person to person, my palms would get sweaty and my heart would pound so hard I thought I would just have a heart attack as it came close to being my turn.

I think God has a great sense of humor. He knows how we are formed, what our weaknesses are, and exactly what it will take to get us to depend on Him. He wants us to be used by Him, but He wants all the glory. So many times He uses our weakness to show His strength. Paul found this out as He asked God to intervene.

> *"Each time he said, 'My grace is all you need. My power works best in weakness.' So now I am glad to boast about my weaknesses, so that the power of Christ can work through me."* 2 Corinthians 12:9 (NLT)

Moment of Decision:

What is something you've said "no" to in the past that you need to reconsider?

Moment of Silence:

Dear Jesus, I know your strength is made perfect in my weakness. Help me, Lord, to be vulnerable enough to let you be strong in me today.

DAY 2

Moment of Truth:

"...let us strip off and throw aside every encumbrance (unnecessary weight) and that sin which so readily (deftly and cleverly) clings to and entangles us, and let us run with patient endurance and steady and active persistence the appointed course of the race that is set before us" Hebrews 12:1 (AMP)

Moment of Reflection:

Earlier in this chapter we talked about the "hand we're dealt." Of all the cards you currently hold in your hand, is each one vitally important to what God has called you to?

Moment of Clarity:

Many times as women, we take on responsibilities that we were never meant to carry. Often, we have the best intentions; we want to help people, and we want to ease the burdens of others.

I mentioned how my husband and I waited 8 years to have children. In all that waiting, I busied myself. I took in stray cats, kittens, dogs, teenagers, and youth pastors. All fine and noble causes. But once God gave me my own children, my hands were no longer able to hold all those other cards. I had to determine which ones God had given me, and which ones I needed to let go of. If I wanted to be really good at what God was calling me to (being a mom), I had to let go of things that weren't as important.

Our number one chief goal is to love the Lord, to worship Him, and to know Him. He gives us the ability to do so many things. Beyond that, God gives us great freedom in choosing our life and our priorities. But some things, while they are not wrong, are not best for us. They divert our attention from what we should be doing and waste our time.

Moment of Decision:

Are you willing to lay aside some things that shouldn't be a priority in your life?

Moment of Silence:

Heavenly Father, help me to see what is important in my life and lay aside those things that slow me down. I want to run my race to the best of my ability, not distracted by things that don't really matter. I want my life to have heavenly significance. Amen.

DAY 3

Moment of Truth:

"But you belong. The Holy One anointed you, and you all know it. I haven't been writing this to tell you something you don't know, but to confirm the truth you do know, and to remind you that the truth doesn't breed lies." 1 John 2:20-21 (MSG)

Moment of Reflection:

Have you ever believed a lie that kept you from pursuing your heart's desire?

Moment of Clarity:

There have been many inventions and changes throughout the course of history that were previously thought to be impossible. A perfect example is what happened to Wilbur Wright.[4] His biography recalls, "'For many years,' he once said, he 'had been afflicted with the belief that flight is possible.'" Even though the rest of the world thought he and his brother were crackpots, and they believed man could not fly, the brothers proved otherwise. In 1903, they proved to the world that, in fact, man can fly. Wilbur knew in his heart what was the truth, and he wouldn't be persuaded by anything contrary.

How often are our dreams kept at bay simply because we have believed faulty information?

I believe that God helps give us guidance and speaks to our hearts about everything. Spiritual and practical alike. Psalm 86:11 tells us, *"Teach me your ways, O Lord, that I may live according to your truth! Grant me purity of heart, so that I may honor you."* (NIV)

We have to remember to align all we hear with the truth of God's Word.

Moment of Decision:

Will you begin to examine the things you've believed that may not be true and re-think some decisions you've made so that you can begin to make better choices?

Moment of Silence:

Dear Lord, I thank you that you have given me your Word. Your word tells me what is true and real. I pray that you will help me begin to make decisions based on scripture, not based on the opinions of people. I trust you to lead me and guide me into all truth. Amen.

DAY 4

Moment of Truth:

"...then he will send the rains in their proper seasons—the early and late rains—so you can bring in your harvests of grain, new wine, and olive oil." Deuteronomy 11:14 (NLT)

Moment of Reflection:

Do you know what season you're in?

Moment of Clarity:

Here in Nevada, we have a saying: If you don't like the weather, wait five minutes; it'll change. When my kids were small, there were seasons that were so unpredictable, they would leave the house in the morning bundled up in winter coats and by afternoon in was nearly 80 degrees.

In life we go through seasons as well. Sometimes the wind shifts before we realize it, at other times the air seems so still and stagnant that we can't wait for it to change.

The Bible talks a lot about seasons. Times of tilling, planting, sowing seed, waiting, watering, and finally, the harvest. I will admit to you, I always wish it were harvest time. In seasons of planting, it's a lot of work with no immediate or measurable reward. In the season of waiting for the harvest it is often boring and tedious. Why can't every day be harvest time - the happy times of scooping up the bounty of God's riches?

But God works through the seasons of our lives. Plowing and preparation as well as rest are vital to the health of our harvest. Even in the seasons we don't particularly like, we can be sure of this; one day, our harvest will come. Be patient as you wait on the harvest in your life. Things are happening under the surface that you cannot yet see.

> *"Dear brothers and sisters, be patient as you wait for the Lord's return. Consider the farmers who patiently wait for the rains in the fall and in the spring. They eagerly look for the valuable harvest to ripen."* James 5:7 (NLT)

Moment of Decision:

Will you determine to walk with grace though your current season?

Moment of Silence:

Dear Jesus, in this season of my life, help me to walk close to you, so that I will have eyes to see what you are doing. Allow me to wait patiently for the harvest as I trust in you for a good crop because I know that you are good. Amen.

DAY 5

Moment of Truth:

"Who shall separate us from the love of Christ? Shall trouble or hardship or persecution or famine or nakedness or danger or sword? No, in all these things we are more than conquerors through him who loved us. For I am convinced that neither death nor life, neither angels nor demons, neither the present nor the future, nor any powers, neither height nor depth, nor anything else in all creation, will be able to separate us from the love of God that is in Christ Jesus our Lord." Romans 8:35, 37-39 (NIV)

Moment of Reflection:

Are you living as a conqueror today?

Moment of Clarity:

We all want to be valiant and strong. We want to live as overcomers, but sometimes we get so bogged down in circumstances that we forget how.

Many times the answer is as simple as stepping away

from the situation for a moment to try to gain better perspective. By spending some time with the Lord in prayer and in reading His Word, we can often hear His voice above the clatter and we can find solutions and hope.

James reminds us how simple it really is.

> *"Come close to God and He will come close to you. [Recognize that you are] sinners, get your soiled hands clean; [realize that you have been disloyal] wavering individuals with divided interests, and purify your hearts [of your spiritual adultery]."*
> James 4:8 (AMP)

The English Standard Version says, "Draw near to God, and He will draw near to you." He really doesn't want you to "do" anything in those moments; He just wants you to "be" with Him. As you are with Him, you are transformed. Not by what you do, but by what He has already done. He loves you so much, and He longs to set you free.

Moment of Decision:

Will you spend some time with Jesus everyday, so that He can make you into the overcomer that you want to be?

Moment of Silence:

Dear Lord, I pray that as I spend time in your presence, you will transform me into your image. Make me new. Give me a fresh perspective that allows me to push past my old excuses and causes me to overcome. I'll take a step toward you today, as you take a step toward me. Thank you for loving me. Amen.

Chapter 4
Made For Moving Forward

S<small>HE WAS</small> down. She was very still. She wasn't doing well. People who knew her the best knew she was not her normal self. She should've been playing with her friends in the Galilean sunshine. She should've been laughing and enjoying life.

Jairus, her daddy, went for help. He was worried. He feared that this might be the end. But he had heard about this man named Jesus who was healing people and setting them free. He saw a huge crowd and knew that must be Him.

He pushed through the crowd and found him. He said, "Please, come heal my daughter!"

They got delayed because more people were pressing in for healing. By the time they got back to the house, they were too late. The mourners had gathered to do what they do. Their presence announced death. "She's gone," they said. "You're too late," they said. "No need to bother the teacher now."

Jesus told Jairus, "Don't fear, just have faith." Jesus made it seem like maybe this was not the end.

They could hear the whispers turn to mocking shrieks of laughter. The mourners' job was to enunciate a hopeless situation, but when hope walked in, they didn't know what to do.

Jesus left the mourners outside and went in with His disciples and the girl's mom and dad. They entered the room where their daughter lay.

This situation found in Mark 5 looked bleak. It looked like it was over. But Jesus didn't speak to what he saw, Jesus gently held her hand, and spoke right to her. He said two words. "Talitha koum."

He said, "Little girl, get up!"

It didn't take a lot of whooping and hollering. It didn't take any fancy tricks. Two words from Jesus got her up!

Can't you imagine the excitement? Can't you picture the joy on her parents faces? Can't you hear the gasps of disbelief from those people gathered outside?

A resurrection! A resurrection of dreams, hopes, potential, and life.

There are times in life when we fear all hope is gone. Maybe you have spiraled so far down into the depths of despair that you can see no way out. Your strength is gone. Your resources are depleted. You are at the end of yourself.

Maybe you are in a place like that right now, and you are reading this book and you say, "I was made for *this* moment? Surely not *this* moment. Something, *anything* else!" I want to assure you, this moment of hopelessness and loss is not the end.

Maybe you feel the mourners surrounding you. They are pronouncing the death of your dreams with great clarity. They reinforce the reality that this is the end of the road.

But it's not the end! It's an invitation to a resurrection.

The End is Not the Last Word

Jesus is the Master of the Resurrection. The whole world thought that when He declared from the cross that "It is finished," that He was done. Gone. Buried. However, He had something amazing in store for the world when He rose from the grave.

What we see isn't always what we get, and the end is not really the end. God gets the last word. When Jesus shouted it is finished, He was saying that part is finished. He lived on in the spirit, He fought death and the grave, He took the keys to hell and He rose victorious! He didn't just do it for those witnesses then, or for that time alone. He rose from the grave for all time, and He arose for us!

> *"And just as Christ was raised from the dead by the glorious power of the Father, now we also may live new lives."* Romans 6:4 (NLT)

That same resurrection power now runs through your veins!

There are times in life when we have to stop listening to the detractors and get up, just because Jesus said we can. He rose from the grave so that we could experience new life. We too, can rise! Why would we choose to waste time listening to the negative noise of naysayers when we have this truth within us?

Holding On To God's Promise

When I became pregnant with my youngest child, I was elated. It was my third child in as many years. My body had gone through a lot in those three years. But I knew this baby was a gift from God. The doctor confirmed my suspicion of pregnancy and the standard tests were scheduled.

When you are newly pregnant, it is all so exciting, and every care is taken to ensure a positive experience. My husband and I went in for our first regular ultrasound. The room had soft lighting, dark wood cabinets, and sweet music was playing in the background. It was beautiful. We were excited to see our baby for the first time.

We quickly noticed a change in the atmosphere. The technician had a very worried look on her face, and the doctor soon came in to tell us they had ordered an internal ultrasound and we would be moved to another room.

I remember it as though I was only a spectator. They ushered us to another room, only it wasn't the warm cushy suite like the last room had been. They moved us into a long white sterile laboratory type of room at the end of the hall. I was on a table in the center of the room. It was cold and quiet. No music played. The lighting was harsh.

They finished conducting the test and the doctor said, "Mrs. Friend, we have some papers for you to sign. We are advising you to abort this fetus. All tests conclude that this baby will have Down's Syndrome, and other complications."

My husband and I didn't even have to consider it. We believed that abortion was wrong, and we knew we had a God that would give us grace to handle whatever may come.

We signed the papers saying that we had received counseling yet refused the recommendations. We walked away from them and left their words of fear and sorrow with them. We didn't believe a word of it. We carried on like all was normal, awaiting the day when we would hold this precious baby, whatever the outcome might be.

I held on to a promise God gave me from Philippians

1:6, *"And I am convinced and sure of this very thing, that He who began a good work in you will continue until the day of Jesus Christ [right up to the time of His return], developing [that good work] and perfecting and bringing it to full completion in you." (AMP)*

I just felt certain that if God started it, He could finish it.

There comes a time when we are faced with a diagnosis, a pink slip, a foreclosure notice, or whatever it may be, and people will render their verdicts upon our situations. It is then that we must walk away from their judgement, their advice, their negativity and begin to hold on to what the Word of God tells us.

The Bible is full of promises, and those promises are for you!

God Waits, But He's Never Late

I walked by faith month by month, carrying that baby. I waited for God to keep His promise to me. Toward the end of my pregnancy, more complications arose. *He who began a good work.* My baby ended up being delivered with great drama three weeks early. *Will continue until the day.* I was in danger and losing consciousness. *Developing that good work.* They rushed my baby out to one room, while rushing me to another, as they worked to stabilize me. *And perfecting.*

When they finally brought little Greyson into my room and laid him in my arms, I knew he was perfect. *And bringing it to full completion.* I knew Jesus had performed a resurrection of my dreams for this child.

Our God has the ability to bring light into situations when they look their darkest.

God never shows up early, and we can trust that He's never too late. But I believe that sometimes He intentionally waits for the situation to get darker so that His glory can be revealed in spectacular fashion.

All through the Bible we see stories like this. Joseph in prison. *God waits.* Daniel in the lion's den. *God waits.* Jonah in the belly of the whale. *God waits.* David running for his life. *God waits.* Lazarus in the tomb. *God waits.* Paul and Silas at trial. *God waits.* Jairus's daughter. *God waits.* Jesus on the cross. *God waits.*

But in each of these situations, God was never late. Because Joseph waited in prison, God positioned him for great influence in the King's palace. Because Daniel was in the lion's den, a whole nation turned to the true and living God. Because Jonah was in the belly of the whale, he was surrendered to the will of God that saved a city. Because David ran for his life, he raised up a mighty army and a kingdom to follow after God. Because Lazarus sat in the tomb, the whole countryside saw the mighty deliverance in the name of Jesus. Because Paul and Silas went through trial, they went to jail and a miracle broke out when angels appeared and the earth shook and the gospel spread. Because Jairus's daughter lay dead, the fame of Jesus burned like wildfire throughout Judea. Because Jesus hung on the cross, He went to the grave, to be risen with victory and healing in His wings!

Because God waits until the perfect moment, He gets the glory!

It's About You, But It's Not For You

When we are in the middle of waiting, it is difficult to see that God is about to break forth into our situation with such glory that everyone will know it could only be God who saved us. We often miss the point, that even in our pain, all of our existence is to bring glory to God. The good times as well as the hard times.

Our life ultimately tells a story. Your story may be about you, but it's really not for you. Your story is meant to mark the way for other people in your world who are desperate to know the way! They need to know what God has done for you. Your resurrection story is what someone else needs to hold on to, to give them faith to move forward.

I once heard the story of Lewis and Clark and all the provisions they took on their journey out west. Along with the trading supplies and survival supplies, they brought a very large supply of ink. They knew that it was vital that they draw new maps and mark all the territory navigated so that others who would follow could find their way. They realized, that it wasn't enough to take the journey, they had to mark the trail.[1]

It is the same for us. It's not enough for us to navigate our life and take the journey. You must mark the trail for future generations! Your story may be about you, but it isn't for you.

Leaving a trail for her children

A Trail To Follow

My journey has not been glamorous or fraught with peril, but it has taught me many lessons. I have learned so much from studying the life and leadership of David because even though he was anointed to lead the people of Israel at a very young age, the process recounted in 1 Samuel was neither swift nor easy.

David was anointed but still just a shepherd boy.

David was destined to wear a crown but herding sheep and protecting them from lions and bears.

David was chosen by God yet left behind by the prophet in Bethlehem.

David had to have been wondering how he would become a mighty king when he was just a country boy who loved good music.

Then one day he was summoned to the king's palace to play for the incredibly grumpy and increasingly dangerous king. He became the best friend of the king's son yet was continually threatened with words as well as with spears. He was running for his life from cave to cave with his true calling on hold for years.

David must've been tempted to think, "If God was in this, it wouldn't be so hard! It must not be right that I step up and take this role," I know I would be tempted to think like that. In all honesty, I have been guilty of thinking things like that. Sometimes when we are striving for a position, a dream or a goal, we mistakenly think that if God were in it, it would be easy. We justify hardship as a sign that God is absent, thinking, "Really? Was God in all of that?"

Do you wonder if David gazed upon his reflection in the pool of water as he bent to get a drink, and asked, "How did I get here? Who am I?"

How did David stay the course through all the roadblocks and twists and turns he found in his journey to his rightful place? How did he find the courage to keep moving forward?

Unwavering Hope

Many of the Psalms were written during these years. In these Psalms, we find the secret of how he did it. David somehow knew the answer to finding his place. The secret was found in trusting God through patient plodding when nothing else made sense.

> *"Lord, my heart is not haughty, nor my eyes lofty; neither do I exercise myself in matters too great or in things too wonderful for me. Surely I have calmed and quieted my soul; like a weaned child with his mother, like a weaned child is my soul within me [ceased from fretting]. O Israel, hope in the Lord from this time forth and forever."* Psalm 131:1-3 (AMP)

This is one of the many Psalms that David wrote, which are referred to as *songs of ascent*. The Hebrew word for ascend is Ma'alah.

When I was in a time of waiting in my life, I fell in love with the concept of this word.

As I researched Ma'alah, I found that it means: Journey to a higher place. Upward. Ascend. Go up. Step by step progression. Walk. To go forward. To live following a certain manner of life. To flow as water. A course of life. Road trodden. A highway. A guiding pillar. Way mark. A goal. A bright object at a distance traveled toward. Zion. A high calling of God.[2]

That is a lot of meaning in one little word. When I discovered this word, I was in a stagnant place stuck between who I was and who I feared becoming. On hold. Tentative. Timid. Unsure. Maybe you've been there. Perhaps you are there right now.

Once I gained this knowledge of who I was and who God was calling me to be, I had to answer the call. Would I be bold? Could I be brave? Did I really trust the Lord to resurrect my life? Did I have it in me to get up?

Look again at David, he wasn't prideful over what he had accomplished so far. "*Lord, my heart is not haughty, nor my eyes lofty;*" He didn't try to over think things and get ahead of himself. "*Neither do I exercise myself in matters too great or in things too wonderful for me.*" He encouraged the people. "*O Israel, hope in the Lord.*" He looked at the concept of time with a long term perspective. "*From this time forth and forever.*"

David found the secret of his "place." It wasn't an end result, he realized it was always about an upward journey. It was about moving forward. He surrendered to the will of God. He maintained focus. He renewed his hope. He built up his relationship with Almighty God, and in that, he became content in his place. (Wherever that place may be at the moment.)

I have tried to follow the trail that David marked out for us, to learn to not think about all the unknowns, to humble and quiet myself by trusting in the Lord. If I am successful at that, I will make the ascent and move forward much more gracefully than clunking around complaining.

Not Going Back

All my life, I was plagued with shyness that felt as though it would overtake me. I would get tightness in my chest and my hands would sweat if I was ever forced to talk. Even while singing on worship teams, I sought invisibility. If someone offered something I wanted, I'd be the last person to raise my hand. If I needed something from God, I'd whisper to him in private rather than shout from the altar.

I felt like I had spent my first forty years waiting, but

I was beginning to be thrust into the spotlight to some extent, by virtue of needs around me. So I followed David. I finally surrendered. I got up. I stepped out. And I began feeling more comfortable and confident in that place. I began taking responsibility for it.

By the time the women's team at my church transitioned into the Legacy team for our third conference, I knew deep down inside that we were on a new ride. This wasn't the same old merry-go-round we were used to, this was going to be a white-knuckle roller coaster kind of ride. We were in a place we'd never been in before. I remember stating so firmly at the prayer huddle before the Legacy Conference in 2011 that this was a new journey we were on and we were not going back! Those words came from my soul as I was realizing what God was telling me. "Daughter, you are in a new place and you are not going back to who you used to be."

The thing with not going back is we have to choose it. It's always easier to stay where we are more comfortable.

I believe that to truly take ground for God and for our own lives we must determine to not go back. Some of us feel good when we are able to stand firm, but we need to go further and take another step! Step out into the unknown and move forward! Unfamiliar territory keeps us on our toes and forces us to focus on what matters. David was able to focus, even when he wasn't where he wanted to be.

I became consumed with such desperate determination to not ever go back to who I used to be. For the first time in my life I understood that *This is my time! I will rise! I will continue to stretch toward what God has for me!*

Whatever It Takes

I became absolutely determined to run after all God had for me. Whatever it takes, became my motto.

Maybe you're like me. Whenever I go to a conference that impacts my life, I want the t-shirt. The t-shirt becomes a tangible reminder of what God is doing in my heart and life. I need tangible reminders. Whether it's writing on my bathroom mirror, scripture cards in my car, words on my office wall, or inspirational jewelry I wear, the power of words is strong. They help me hold on to truth from God's Word in me. But at this point in my life, I needed something more. I needed to be marked.

Marked

By now you must be wondering what I did. Yes, it was desperate. Some would say it was foolish. I wanted the word Ma'alah tattooed on my body.

Say what? A middle aged, conservative, small town, sweet and quiet pastor's wife wanted a tattoo?

No. A passionate, determined, purposeful, resolute, tenacious woman of God wanted a tattoo. I was willing to do whatever it took to gain a little forward momentum in my life.

I'm not marking this part of my trail to argue the pros and cons of tattooing. There are plenty of other places to research such information. If you're interested, one of the most interesting ones I found was actually on YouTube by Pastor Craig Groeschel where he answers the question, "Can a Christian Get a Tattoo?"[3] Whether or not you agree with it, let's set those issues aside for the sake of hearing my tale. This became the next step in my journey. I was sure.

I researched artists. I found the Hebrew style of calligraphy I wanted. I knew which way I wanted it oriented on my wrist so that I could always read it and be reminded to keep journeying to a higher place. I went to the shop and interviewed the big scary tattoo dude. I was a little freaked out, but I paid my deposit. I made the appointment. I waited.

I told very few people of my crazy plan. When the day of my appointment came, a friend came with me. The artist had me sign the forms, approve the artwork and size, and we were ready to go.

I laid back on the table, offering my left arm to the artist's needle. My friend sat on my right so I could be distracted from the pain. We chatted the entire time. It went so fast! In 30 minutes it was done and bandaged up, and I was on my way out the door.

They told me to wait three hours before removing the wrapping. I was so excited. I felt like a kid waiting for Christmas!

Finally, three hours later, I got to unwrap the bandage and see my decision *in the flesh*!

How can this be? What trauma! What a tragedy! I was trembling with the startling realization.

It was upside down!

Upside Down, But Right Side Out

Seriously? After all my efforts to do it just right? After facing all my fears? I am one of those horrible tattoo-gone-wrong statistics?

My inner dialog was screaming, "This tattoo was to remind myself of my transformation! This was for me! I did this so I could remind myself to keep moving forward, and it's upside down? Really?!"

After I began to calm down and recovered from the initial shock, I could hear Him gently speaking to my spirit. He said, "Connie, your story is not for you." As I extended my hand, I realized, others could see it perfectly.

Isn't that just like God? The story I thought was for me, wasn't. The tattoo I designed for me, isn't. My story, just like yours, is designed to be told. And now, every day, I am reminded to tell my story.

Your story may be about you, but it isn't for you. Maybe it's time for you to get up. Let God begin to resurrect what you thought was dead. It is time for you to hold on to hope. Stop waiting and start marking the trail for someone else.

Your legacy is all about equipping those around you. It's about reaching for the hand of one in the next generation and sharing your story to enrich their life. There are others who need your voice. They are waiting for your experience to transform their future. Reach. Share. Tell.

Your story may look upside down to you, but it will be perfectly right side up to the one who needs to hear it. You were made for this moment.

Sheri's Story
In Her Own Words

One year ago this month I was at the Legacy Conference, and I remember standing and praying and telling God, "I don't want to sit quiet anymore. I want more, God!" That night my life changed! A passion unlike anything I had ever known was born in me. Up until that moment, I never understood what it meant to have a passion for anything.

One month later, I became a founding member of Our Time Rising, a mentoring program for girls aged 18-23. Founding this awesome ministry is not the only change that has taken place since my transforming moment with God.

I never had a relationship with my mom, and I never thought I could have one. My mom was an alcoholic and my step dad was abusive. As a kid, I had to go live with my grandparents, so for many years I was angry with my mom. Over a year ago I moved my grams to Carson City and it was a tough time for me. I had to start talking to my mom, and as things changed between us, I knew that I had to forgive her. I told her that I was angry with her and she knew why. As we shared things about our lives and cried together, the healing took place. I am here to say I have forgiven my mom.

The other part of my story just happened a few months ago. Since my husband Mark and I have been married I have never had a good relationship with his kids' mother (Mark's ex-wife), and rightfully so. Every past comes with baggage and lots of things happened that made the relationship stressful. A time came when we had to talk. In doing that I started to share things about what God was doing in my life. With each continuing conversation, we began to have understanding, and a friendship was formed. Today I can say that we are friends and our stressful relationship has been healed. We pray for each other and I truly am amazed by what God can do when we open the door just a little. I can say she is my friend. I can also tell you that I was also able to forgive myself and both of these things are huge!

I shared these things to let you know there are greater things in store for us when we tell God, "I want more." I won't sit quiet ever again. These were the areas that God helped me through. I believe God is a God of RESTORATION. I have relationships that are restored. My identity has been restored. My marriage is being restored.

My past is not my story. My story is what I'm doing now. I will stand up and be bold. I won't be shy because that has kept me from so many things that God wanted to do in my life. It's time for turning points for each of us. If you know that you need to restore broken relationships let God help you do it. It's time! It truly is Our Time!

Defining Moments In Your Day

DAY 1

Moment of Truth:

"The tongue can bring death or life; those who love to talk will reap the consequences." Proverbs 18:21 (NLT)

Moment of Reflection:

Has anyone spoken negative words over you?

Moment of Clarity:

When we are in a difficult place, it becomes vital to our health and our outlook to stay surrounded by positive people. When the children of Israel escaped the clutches of the Egyptian task masters, they were free, and it should have taken them no more than eight days to enter the promised land. Negativity, grumbling and complaining brought one trouble upon them after another.

After forty years of wandering, God had seen a pattern. When He gave them the green light to enter the promised land, He gave explicit instruction. He told them to circle the city of Jericho one time each day for six days. Then on the seventh day, they were to march around seven times. However, they were to do it in *silence*.

Remember: when Jesus healed the little girl, He left the naysayers outside. God knows the power of words in our lives. Do you? Limit negativity. Stay away from the ones who would announce your doom. Don't listen to it. Run from it.

Moment of Decision:

How will you protect yourself from harmful words?

Moment of Silence:

Father, help me to protect what I allow into my spirit by the words I listen to, and remind me to choose my own words wisely. Help me to choose life. Amen.

DAY 2

Moment of Truth:

"So let's not get tired of doing what is good. At just the right time we will reap a harvest of blessing if we don't give up." Galatians 6:9 (NLT)

Moment of Reflection:

Have you been tempted to give up too soon?

Moment of Clarity:

Perspective is a beautiful thing. Life would be so much easier if we all had hindsight. When we absolutely can't see the future, trusting in man will only get us so far. Trusting in the Lord becomes our only true hope.

When I was nineteen years old and my husband and I were youth pastors in Alaska, it became common for us to fly in tiny four seater planes. These planes didn't have fancy guidance systems. We had to trust our pilot to fly by what he could see. It was very scary when the clouds rolled in and visibility was decreased. Frankly, I didn't want to trust the guy in the front seat.

I'd much rather fly on a 747 jumbo jet, where they have such advanced guidance systems that the pilots aren't required to see a thing. They just trust the instruments. I don't get nervous flying on 747's. Getting to my destination is pretty much a sure thing.

Trusting the Lord is a sure thing too. We don't need to see the future if we just rely on and trust in Him. Just because we can't see how to get to our destination doesn't mean we stop our journey prematurely. It means we hold on to our dreams and trust God to get us there.

Moment of Decision:

What dream do you need to hold on to a little longer?

Moment of Silence:

Jesus, help me to relinquish my need to control and to just sit back and enjoy the ride. I know I can trust you, and I thank you for knowing the way. I know you are the way. I will rest in that today.

DAY 3

Moment of Truth:

"Guide older women into lives of reverence so they end up as neither gossips nor drunks, but models of goodness. By looking at them, the younger women will know how to love their husbands

and children, be virtuous and pure, keep a good house, be good wives. We don't want anyone looking down on God's Message because of their behavior." Titus 2:3-5 (MSG)

Moment of Reflection:

Is there someone in your life who has marked the trail for you?

Moment of Clarity:

Naomi paved the way for Ruth, Elizabeth helped guide Mary, and Jesus trained all twelve disciples. Psalm 145:4 reminds us, *"Let each generation tell its children of your mighty acts; let them proclaim your power."* (NLT) It is God's plan that we help make a way for those who follow us.

I intentionally look for healthy, vibrant women to pattern myself after. But frankly, there have been times when I couldn't find any. If that seems to be the case for you, don't let that stop you. There are so many fantastic women leaders that you can follow via the Internet. Women like Joyce Meyer, Bobbie Houston, Lisa Bevere, Christine Caine, Charlotte Scanlon Gambill, and Holly Wagner. They are available on all the social media sites and they all have books available. Read, grow, allow yourself to be influenced and mentored from afar. And keep looking for those nearby. If you look for them, you will find them.

Moment of Decision:

Will you add one person of influence to your life today?

Moment of Silence:

Dear Lord, I pray that you will bring good, positive, healthy women into my life who will help guide me and influence me to become more like you. Help me to see them, and help me to be one to someone else. Amen.

DAY 4

Moment of Truth:

"Friends, don't get me wrong: By no means do I count myself an expert in all of this, but I've got my eye on the goal, where God is beckoning us onward-to Jesus. I'm off and running, and I'm not turning back." Philippians 3:13-14 (MSG)

Moment of Reflection:

What would you identify as the next step for you as you journey upward?

Moment of Clarity:

Thomas Watson, founder of IBM, once said, "There is no such thing as standing still. You cannot stay in one place: you either go forward or go backward."

It is often, so much more comfortable to stay where you are, but God's plans for you are so much bigger than for your comfort. God wants you to have a big life full of fresh color, excitement, and adventure. It takes some amount of boldness and courage to step out, to get up from where you are, but the pay off is so worth it.

In the book, *The Circle Maker*, Mark Batterson writes, "He wants to take you places you have never been...but if you want God to do something new in your life, you can't do the same old thing."[4]

Moment of Decision:

Are you willing to take a step today? What will it be?

Moment of Silence:

Dear Jesus, as I have faith to step out in boldness, I pray that you will go with me. Your Word says that you will never leave me nor forsake me, and I pray that I will feel your presence go with me. Thank you for always nudging me forward. I want to get up! Amen.

DAY 5

Moment of Truth:

"And we know that God causes everything to work together for the good of those who love God and are called according to his purpose for them." Romans 8:28 (NLT)

Moment of Reflection:

Is there a situation in your life that feels completely upside down to you?

Moment of Clarity:

I love the fact that in God's economy, nothing goes to waste. Even things that we regret can be used to help someone else, to the glory of God. It's a relief to know that we serve a God who is that kind.

Ephesians 1:10-11 tells us, *"And this is the plan: At the right time he will bring everything together under the authority of Christ—everything in heaven and on earth. Furthermore, because we are united with Christ, we have received an inheritance from God, for he chose us in advance, and he makes everything work out according to his plan."* (NLT)

Did you catch that? He makes *everything* work out. Wrongs can be made right, sorrow can be turned to joy, and things that look dead can be brought to life! Jesus, who has power over death and the grave, has power over every situation we face.

Moment of Decision:

Will you trust Jesus with every part of your life, even the parts that don't make sense?

Moment of Silence:

Dear Heavenly Father, You know about _____ .
You know how I've tried to make sense of it, and on my own, I just don't see how any good can come from it. Today, I choose to give it to you. I pray that you will make something beautiful from it, and as I release it to you, I pray that you will give me your complete peace. In Jesus' name, Amen.

Chapter 5
Made For Position

A FEW YEARS ago, when my kids were in middle school, I accompanied them on a school trip to China. On one leg of the trip, the tour allowed us a short shopping excursion in Shanghai. A bus dropped us off in an area filled with open air markets. My daughter and I somehow got separated from the rest of the group, and we soon realized that with each little alley we went down, we got deeper and deeper into a labyrinth of the sights and smells and sounds of this foreign land. We walked. We looked. We searched. We saw nothing and no one that looked familiar to us. There were raw carcasses hanging in booths…heads and beaks and claws. There were people selling things and pushing their goods into us, there were strange smells and steam, and as the clock ticked closer to our departure time, the worse our fears and imaginings and sweating became.

Lost

I didn't want to tell my little girl we were lost, but one look at her face and I knew I didn't have to. Her eyes were huge!

I wouldn't look at her more than a second, I didn't want her to see the near panic in my face. I grabbed hold of her little hand and and trudged on. Turning corner after corner until everything looked the same.

We eventually stumbled out into the street, and there off in the distance, we saw the youth pastor - a big white American in a bright yellow shirt. We waved, "We're here! We're here!"

We weren't lost any more. *Whew!* I don't know if I've ever been that fearful of being lost, except maybe in the grocery store when I was five. We needed GPS.

Global Positioning System

GPS. Global Positioning System. GPS is now available everywhere. In every phone, in every car, on any computer. It's so great! I don't know how I ever survived without it.

It's really important to know where you are. When you're at the mall, and you can't find your bearings, you can go up to one of those big murals that has all the stores mapped out on it, and you can always find the arrow that says, "You are here." It lets you know how to look for everything else.

By now, as you have been reading this book, you've had time to consider where you are, and where you might be going, but you might be wondering if there is any way to get into position so you're ready for what God has prepared for you. I believe there is!

I believe God has a beautiful design for each person's life, and with every decision we make, we either get ourselves in position for the next big thing, or we step out of position. Jeremiah 29:11 assures us, *"For I know the plans I have for you,' says the Lord . 'They are plans for good and not for disaster, to give you a future and a hope.'"* (NLT) But God leaves it up to us to acquire as much blessing as we choose by the position we get into.

Our lives must intersect with His will, which makes it vital that we stay in position!

The Wrong Place at the Wrong Time

Okay, I understand this story is going to date me, but when I was a young teenager, I was asked to sing a solo with a one-hundred-voice youth choir from my home church at a Jesus Festival in the Pacific Northwest. It was the late 1970's and many famous bands, preachers, and musicians were slated to be there.

I was almost fifteen years old. My choir director asked me to sing the song that James Taylor made famous, *You've Got A Friend*. I lacked self confidence, and my shyness consumed me. I was so terrified that I made myself sick and didn't even show up!

If that had been my child, I would've given a severe time of "instruction" about that mistake. What a wasted opportunity! I was being set up for an amazing experience. God had gifts waiting for me in that opportunity, and I clearly stepped out of position.

I didn't get to meet all the great people my fellow choir members met. I didn't get to sing a solo in front of a crowd of 20,000 people. I missed out. I messed up. I've often wondered what hardship that decision caused for other people. My choir director, my youth pastor, the girl who had to take my place. Was I seen as a flake and a loser? Maybe. Weak and confused? Maybe. In the wrong place at the wrong time? For sure!

Anything that keeps us from being in the right place at the right time, is the wrong place to be!

Disobedience is often the culprit that takes us out of

position while faithfulness is the key to being in the right place at the right time.

David's Stepping Stones

The Biblical character David is so widely known because of his courageous exploits. No one would deny his fearless determination as he faced down the giant, Goliath on the battlefield before all of Israel.

The entire Philistine Army had been shouting and taunting the Army of Israel. For forty days, the giant yelled and screamed his threats before the army of God. The men of Israel were rattled and worn. Exhausted, hungry, and in fear of defeat, young David arrived with food. He asked, "What's the big deal, fella's, I'll kill the giant for you, no problem!" His brothers were appalled at his bravado! "Who does he think he is?!" David was in position.

What they didn't know was David had been on a path, jumping from one stepping stone to the next, with faithful obedience each step of the way. Let's look back at those stones that got him in position.

> But David persisted. *"'I have been taking care of my father's sheep and goats,' he said. 'When a lion or a bear comes to steal a lamb from the flock, I go after it with a club and rescue the lamb from its mouth. If the animal turns on me, I catch it by the jaw and club it to death. I have done this to both lions and bears, and I'll do it to this pagan Philistine, too, for he has defied the armies of the living God! The Lord who rescued me from the claws of the lion and the bear will rescue me from this Philistine!' Saul finally consented. 'All right,*

*go ahead,' he said. 'And may the Lord be with you!'"*1 Samuel 17:34-37 (NLT)

He did whatever he was asked to do. *Stepping stone.*
  He took good care of his fathers flocks. *Stepping stone.*
    He killed lions. *Stepping stone.*
      He overcame bears. *Stepping stone.*
        Rescued the sheep. *Stepping stone.*
          His father, told him to check on his brothers.
          Stepping stone.
              Honor the name of the Lord. *Stepping stone.*
              Slay the giant.

That encounter with the giant didn't just happen, and David being prepared for such a traumatic event wasn't an accident. Each stepping stone brought him closer to the position God wanted him to be in to receive all that God planned to give him: a wife, a kingdom, and a legacy.

Taking steps together

What If's

Maybe you are like me, and you play with "what if" scenarios in your head. What if I hadn't said no to so many opportunities when I was young and stupid. What if I hadn't gone to Northwest University in 1982? Who would I have married, and what would my kids be like? What if I had said no to Jesus when I was a child? Where would I be now?

Now that I'm older and I have more experience and I know what I know, I am much more conscious of the weight of every decision. I'm much more concerned with the position each choice puts me in. I say no less, and I say yes more.

What if you said yes to Jesus? What if you followed Him more passionately? Would you be in a different position a year from now than where you are today? What if you studied harder in school? What if you dreamed a bigger dream? What if you prayed a larger prayer? What if you behaved like the person you want to be? What position would you be in?

So much in our lives is a result of positioning. Being at the right place at the right time. Doing the best things at the best times. Being faithful. Being prepared. Like GPS guides a car, our lives intersect with God's plan when we position ourselves well.

Last fall, I drove my daughter from Nevada to Missouri to start her new life at a new school, in a new church, and with new people surrounding her. It certainly felt like a destiny-driven trip. I could sense that more was happening than what was really happening. Through detours and road construction, we were getting her in position for something amazing.

Maybe you've felt that in your life things are clicking, momentum is yours; you are in position for a big promotion, or an answer to prayer, or a financial windfall. Faithful obedience is what gets us there by following each stepping stone no matter how hard it is or how long it takes.

Where Jesus is, is where I want to be just like the woman in Mark 5 with the issue of blood. She knew she had to get in position. She pressed through the crowds and the busyness of the street because she knew if she could just get close enough to Him, she could be healed. It wasn't easy. What if she hadn't heard about Jesus? What if she hadn't believed? What if she hadn't pressed through? What if she hadn't gotten into position? It took twelve years of suffering before her opportunity to get in position arrived and changed her in an instant.

Salvation Is Here

When you think back to the moment you accepted Christ, is it a surprise that He found you? Or do you look back at your life and see how He was positioning you to find Him because He knew where you were all along?

There's a story in Luke 19 that is about a man named Zacchaeus. Zacchaeus was despised because he was a tax collector, and he was also very short. I'm sure no one was eager to do him any favors to help him see above the crowds. Zacchaeus decided to put himself into a better position to see Jesus, so he climbed up a tree.

Jesus saw that Zacchaeus put himself out there, that he did something no one else did, and He took note. Jesus responded, *"Salvation has come to this home today, for this man has shown himself to be a true son of Abraham. For the Son of Man came to seek and save those who are lost."* Luke 19:9-10 (NLT)

Zacchaeus met with destiny that day. Jesus told him, salvation is *here*! Zacchaeus recognized his lostness, and he put himself in position to be found.

Sometimes we have a tendency to wallow, to stay in our place of want or need, and to wait for rescue. But what God is waiting for is to see us get ourselves into position to receive what He has for us.

Two Kids From Ohio

I know of a woman who was raised in a little town in Ohio in the 1940's. While our country was still reeling from the Great Depression and World War II was happening on the global stage, this little girl was growing up in a home where her father had abandoned the family. Her mother simply did not have enough money to support the family, so she and her brothers were sent away to live in foster care while her mom looked for work in factories.

This little girl was shuffled from place to place, being abused along the way, until the time came when her mother could get her children back. By the time she was in high school, she realized she needed to pay her own way, so she eventually dropped out of school to get her own job. This teenage girl found her way to a church where she was wonderfully saved, and that is where her life really began. She put herself in position to meet up with God. She was beginning to gain perspective, to survey the landscape, and to see where she was. Little did she know, she was positioning herself for so much more.

At the same time, a little boy was growing up in a neighboring town in Ohio. He was living in a home where his father had abandoned the family as well. He lived a harsh life where he was often beaten by those who should have cared for him the most. He began to work hard from a very young age and realized he wanted out of where he was.

He quit school after 6th grade, and he began doing any kind of manual labor work he could get. In that era, the

U.S. government was always looking for healthy young men to enlist in the armed services, so he lied about his age and joined the Navy before he was even eighteen years old. He was stationed in Hawaii and began making new friends. Some of his buddies invited him to go to church. He was putting himself in position, and there, he met God. He discovered that he was loved by God and adopted as His own son! How amazing.

Transplanted

The young man eventually made his way back to Ohio, and he positioned himself in a church. He wanted more of God, but he got so much more. He also found a sweet girlfriend in the little church he attended. Yes, the same girl I told you about earlier. Putting themselves in position to meet with God actually positioned them for more than they could have imagined!

They started out simply wanting a place to belong. They wanted the security of a family. They positioned themselves in a church family where they became transplanted from abandonment to adoption. Psalm 92:13 says, *"For they are transplanted to the Lord's own house. They flourish in the courts of our God."* (NLT)

When we are faithfully obedient to place ourselves in a position covered by God's grace, He is so aware of what we need, and He longs to give us the desires of our hearts even when we aren't quite sure what they are. When we choose to remain firmly planted, our lives begin to flourish.

This couple found grace in the church. *Stepping stone.*

They found each other in the church. *Stepping stone.*

They served God together in the church. *Stepping stone.*

They got married in the church. *Stepping stone.*

They began to believe that God had marvelous plans for their lives. *Stepping stone*
They felt like they were positioned for anything!

They weren't content with staying the same or being surrounded by the same people that had always brought them down. They decided to do something remarkable.

Into The Vast Unknown

They were ready to face their giant. They pulled up roots and left behind everyone they ever knew and everything familiar they had ever known, and they went clear across the country as far as they could possibly go until they reached the ocean. A new longing required a new position. They left abandonment. They left abuse. They left brokenness and bad memories. They left unhealthy connections with the people in their past. They chose a new way of life. New connections. New relationships. New life.

Like Zacchaeus, they had a need; they longed for a better vantage point, so they put themselves in position for Jesus to meet their need. He climbed a tree. They went to Oregon.

Because of their decision to position themselves into God's plan, their children never knew abuse, or shame, or abandonment, or fear. The curse of the past had been broken. The two kids from Ohio are my parents, and I will be forever grateful that they got in position for God to change their destiny because it also changed mine. And because they chose to position themselves in the place of promise, they built a legacy for generations to come.

Already, God is placing new dreams in your heart as you read this book. They may even be dreams you thought were long dead, but they are being reawakened right now.

You may be wondering exactly what are some steps you can take to get in position. I want to give you some stepping stones to follow that will help you become positioned for more in your life.

Slippery Rocks and Deep Water

When I was nineteen years old, I married my husband. I was completely naive and unprepared for the life of adventure he wanted to live. Just before graduating from Northwest University, we accepted our first position as youth pastors in a church in Sitka, Alaska. Every day off my husband had, he spent in the wilderness. He loved fishing, hunting and exploring. I, on the other hand, would not give up my high heals or dresses. I did give in and buy some heavy duty hiking boots.

One day he convinced me to go fishing with him. To me, fishing didn't mean actually fishing. It meant following along the river's edge, fighting off hordes of diabolical mosquitos by the thousands, looking over my shoulder for bears, and fearing for my life because of the countless oceanic creatures lurking at the mouth of the river. Not at all my idea of a fun time, but I considered it to be my wifely duty. I mean, what did I know? I was nineteen!

He just loved fishing these wild untouched streams. He would think like the fish, and go where they would go. At one point, he said, "Let's cross the river and fish from the other aside!"

Say what? It's one river! Aren't the fish on that side of the river the same as the fish on this side?

I was worried because number one, I couldn't swim very well. Number two, I didn't want my new boots to get wet. Number three, it was cold water! Not to mention, I just thought it was a dumb idea.

He persisted.

He said he would give me a piggy back ride while I held his fishing pole in one hand and his tackle box in the other. He swore he wouldn't drop me. I reluctantly climbed on.

I could feel his feet shuffling through the rocky bottom of the river, finding the right rocks to stand on. He was searching for stepping stones. When we were about mid way across the river, I felt him step forward and I leaned forward with him as he strained for a foot hold, but his foot just kept going. It seemed like a sudden drop off and we both toppled into the middle of the rushing Alaskan river. I was sputtering and straining. All I heard from my husband was, "Don't drop the gear!"

I began to bob my way down river crying and gasping

as I went. My hands were full, so I couldn't paddle. My feet were weighed down by my brand new, heavy duty hiking boots. I was trying to breathe but I was panicking. I noticed that he was not with me! What is going on, I wondered. I could hear him yelling. The rapids were ahead, and I could see the ocean getting closer, this was it! I just knew it! "I am dying," I thought. I kept hearing him yelling. What was he saying?

"STAND UP!"

Oh. For real? Stand up? I should have known. How embarrassing and maddening at the same time. Ridiculous! I stood up. My teal green sweats sagged heavy, I was drenched and shivering head to toe. But I was alive!

Sometimes we get in the flurry of life happening all around us and we forget the basics. We feel like we are fighting for our lives trying to breathe, and we need to be reminded. We need to have some solid ground under our feet. Stand up, girl, stand up. Step on the stones of what you already know.

What Do You Know?

When we are trying to grow and stretch our capacity we sometimes forget the very basic things that brought us to where we are. There are three really important things we know we should do, but if we forget to do them, we could find ourselves drowning and overwhelmed.

The first thing we know to do is to read His Word. The Bible is God's gift of life to us. It reveals His thoughts and His ways on paper for us to carry around with us. It doesn't just *represent* life, it doesn't just *hold* life, it *is* life. In Hebrews 4:12 it explains, *"For the word of God is alive and powerful. It is sharper than the sharpest two-edged sword, cutting between soul and spirit, between joint and marrow. It exposes our innermost thoughts and desires."* (NLT) When we don't read His word, we underestimate the power that is found within its pages. We position ourselves for wisdom when we read His word.

The second thing we know is that it's important to go to church. It grows us and builds stability into our character when we are faithful to attend church. The Bible tells us how important it is that we gather together, *"And let us not neglect our meeting together, as some people do, but encourage one another, especially now that the day of his return is drawing near."* Hebrews 10:25 (NLT)

Ephesians 5 explains how Jesus actually died for the church, how the church is the bride of Christ, and how Jesus and the church are one. If He cares that much for the church, shouldn't it be important to us? The enemy wants to keep us separate from one another. He wants to keep us isolated. But when we gather together, there is strength. When we come to His house, we hear clear answers to the questions we are asking. We position ourselves for life when we are planted in the house.

The third thing we know to do is to love one another. The Bible is pretty blatant about it. *"So now I am giving you a new commandment: Love each other. Just as I have loved you, you should love each other."* (John 13:34 NLT) Most of us can probably recite a passage or two from the Bible about how important it is that we love. Did you know that in Proverbs 14:22 it says, *"Those who plan what is good, find love and faithfulness."* We all want that, right?

William Wordsworth said, "The little unremembered acts of kindness and love are the best parts of a person's life."

Sometimes we need to stop justifying why people do or do not deserve love and simply love just because He said to. Love as though you expect nothing in return. But here's the thing about love. It always does return. It may not be in the way we expect or in the time we anticipate, but it always returns. Luke 6:38 says, "*Give, and it will be given to you. A good measure, pressed down, shaken together and running over, will be poured into your lap. For with the measure you use, it will be measured to you.*" (NIV) We position ourselves for fulfillment when we love one another.

Who Is In Your World?

Let's face it, some people are connected to us out of choice, and others have simply settled into our airspace, and we have accepted the notion that we have no choice in it. We have been taught from an early age to be accommodating - to never be rude. Whether they are related by marriage, by blood, or friendship, they are connected to us whether we like it or not. There comes a time when we need to take an honest assessment of who is in our life and take steps to either claim it or to change it. Taking responsibility for who is in your would could change everything.

My mother had many words of warning, maybe yours did to. She'd say things like, "You are who your friends are," "Those who lie down with dogs wake up with fleas," and "Don't cast your pearls to swine." Proverbs 12:26 says, "*The righteous choose their friends carefully, but the way of the wicked leads them astray.*" (NIV)

If you have friends that are not lifting you up or helping propel you forward, then you should seriously consider getting some new friends that will! I'm not saying you should "break up" with all your old friends. I'm saying to be wise enough to limit your exposure to them and make certain that you are the one setting the tone and temperature of your moments together.

I went through a growth period in my life where I literally had to choose. I knew that God had chosen me, and

I knew He had called me. His Word declared to me that I am the light in this dark world. I am the salt in a tasteless world. But as long as I allowed others to throw their blanket of negativity and doubt over me, I would not shine. As long as I allowed people to neutralize me, I could not be salty. I had to stay the same, or take action and choose to rise.

I kept a card on my bathroom counter for months that simply had one word on it. I looked at it every day. It gave me more courage than I can explain. It helped a spine of steel to develop within me. One word gave me strength to change.

RISE.

Our relationships with people can actually be a form of bondage where their words of unbelief and negativity can feel like chains around our feet. At one point I had to face the person who had the biggest negative hold on me. I looked them straight in the eye and declared, "I will rise!" And just like that, it was broken. I found out it wasn't really their problem after all; it was mine. I had allowed that bondage; I had allowed my fear to have a grip on my life. Once I chose to be free, I was!

You might be thinking, what about my mother-in-law!? It's not like I can dump her!

That's true. That is the time you ask God for more grace, more patience, more wisdom, and you practice guarding your heart. Proverbs 4:23 tells us, *"Above all else, guard your heart, for everything you do flows from it."* (NIV)

Refuse to allow negativity or harsh or unkind words to penetrate your heart. Get filled up with God and there will be very little room left over for extraneous nonsense to hang around.

Invest in new friends. Go to places where good people go. Make the effort to make a new friend. In the last chapter,

I listed some great leaders to follow. You can make virtual friends! I find tons of inspiration from leaders I follow on twitter. I find encouragement and prayer support from friends on Facebook. Don't tell me you can't find inspirational connections. Because it's easier than ever nowadays.

Trust God With What You Don't Know

Sometimes it's reassuring to know you're not supposed to feel truly comfortable. Jesus didn't come to make us comfortable, He came to set us on mission! Comfort is often way overrated. That desire for comfort alone can hold us captive if we let it.

Alan Cohen said this: "It takes a lot of courage to release the familiar and seemingly secure, to embrace the new. But there is no real security in what is no longer meaningful. There is more security in the adventurous and exciting, for in movement there is life, and in change there is power."[1]

Choosing courage over comfort is something I think we get better at with practice. I think back again to the story of the children of Israel when they were still slaves in Egypt. They complained and cried out to God for change in their circumstances. God was aware of their position and He heard their prayers, yet God didn't do it for them. He provided an answer. The answer was somewhere else. Somewhere over "there." They had to get into a new position. He told them to get moving, to go to the promised land. Once they took a step toward their new place, they got just part of the way there, they got discouraged and uncomfortable, and they grumbled and begged for the familiar. They refused to take the next step. The people said, *"'If only the Lord had killed us back in Egypt,' they moaned. 'There we sat around pots filled with meat and ate all the bread we wanted. But now you have brought us into this wilderness to starve us all to death.'"* Exodus 16:3 (NLT)

Isn't it interesting that if we are not careful, our present place of discomfort and anxiety can distort the memory of the recent past. (Even if it was really, really bad!)

We need to remember that even though circumstances change, our God never changes. Hebrews 13:8 says, *"Jesus Christ is the same, yesterday and today and forever."* (NLT) Our God is good and caring and loving and strong and powerful. The God that took the Israelites out of slavery is the same God who will move us out of our circumstances. The God who parted the Red Sea is the same God who will make a way for you. The God that provided for their needs is the same God that will provide for yours. The God who saved my parents back in Ohio is the same God who will be faithful to lead my children in the future. I can almost hear God saying, "Stop complaining. Take the next step! Pick up your feet and walk already!"

We position ourselves to receive what He has promised when we trust Him.

Just like the children of Israel, we have to learn to trust God - to obey him. It took forty years for them to get "there." It has been speculated that the journey should've taken a few days. A very few days! They stubbornly refused to get into position to receive their promise for 40 years!

Maybe you can relate to that journey? We would be wise to learn this matter of trust quickly so that we can get into position to receive what God has promised.

Proverbs 3:5 says, *"Trust God from the bottom of your heart; don't try to figure out everything on your own. Listen for God's voice in everything you do, everywhere you go; he's the one who will keep you on track."* (MSG)

You were made for this moment.

Gere's Story
In Her Own Words

I was born into a family where both parents loved me. I was secure and happy. One of my favorite things as a little girl was spending time with my dad; I just thought he hung the moon. One day when I was 14 years old, I was home alone with my dad, and he suffered a severe heart attack right in front of me and fell to the kitchen floor. Right there in the middle of our kitchen, my dad died in my arms, and my life changed.

My mother remarried eleven months later, but the man that she married didn't want children. I was placed into foster care. I was moved through eight homes in two years. I became filled with feelings of insecurity, fear, and abandonment.

I eventually grew up and struck out on my own, just doing the best I could. I got a job as a teller at a bank in Modesto, California. One day, a man named James came in and asked me out on a date. He introduced me to Jesus and the trajectory of my life was shifted. I said "Yes" to God and "Yes" to James, who became my husband.

I began going to church and raising two step sons, and then God blessed me with my own beautiful son. We loved taking missions trips to various parts of the world. I started my own basket design business, and life was good. I had spent many years rebuilding a relationship with my mom and step dad. As only God could orchestrate, we lived many years with them in our lives. I expected us to live happily ever, and we did, for 23 years.

The year my son was about to leave home for college, my mother passed away. Because of the past brokenness that we had worked so hard to mend, her death was especially painful. It seemed to dig up old wounds. The grief was putting me in at fog at times, but I was trusting the Lord to carry me through.

Just a few months later, my son moved to Southern

California to attend a Christian university. Two weeks later, one morning as my husband was getting ready for work, he came upstairs to bring me coffee, and he suffered a fatal heart attack and went to be with the Lord right there next to the bed.

I was truly devastated. Feelings of abandonment, fear, and insecurity resurfaced and left me feeling hopeless and so very alone. How could I do this? I had a son to get through college. I had my husband's business to figure out what to do with. I had choices to make, and I had a lot of excuses to weed through. I was unqualified. I was afraid. I was alone.

But I decided I didn't have to stay alone. I could let people in. So I allowed myself to be surrounded by strong Christian friends. I went to counseling. I got myself out of bed most days.

I felt that the Lord wanted me to continue my husband's business. After all, it was his legacy. It was his business that funded the mission endeavors that I loved so much, but I had no idea how to do it. I didn't know anything about gaskets or about running a manufacturing plant. But I knew people. So I asked for help, I found mentors, I sought wise council, and one day at a time, I rose.

My son now has graduated from college with a music degree, and he leads worship at a Saddleback Church. The business that James started is now my business, and we are having our most successful year ever. This year I funded my first, but not my last, water well in Ghana, Africa.

I know I had every reason to make excuses. Nobody would have blamed me for curling up in a ball and giving up. But I heard God whisper, even in my moments of despair, that He had more for me. One day at a time, He provided me with fresh hope. I understand that if God calls me, He will make me able. I listened. I obeyed. I wouldn't have believed it, but I was made for this moment.

Defining Moments In Your Day

DAY 1

Moment of Truth:

"The Lord directs the steps of the godly. He delights in every detail of their lives." Psalm 37:23 (NLT)

Moment of Reflection:

Have you ever been in the wrong place at the wrong time?

Moment of Clarity:

We often reflect on the above verse from Psalm 37:23, and we know that God directs the steps of the godly. It's an absolute truth that we can rely on. I think where we sometimes get into trouble is we forget to consult God. We get busy, and we think what we are doing is good, but often we overlook constant communication with God that could keep our hearts and minds in check.

When God has told us what he wants us to do, we need to do the whole thing, not start it, feel a little bit good about ourselves, and call it good. Partial obedience is not only dangerous to us, it is disobedience to God. Finish the job He has asked you to do.

If we are truly godly, we will listen to Him and we will follow through.

Moment of Decision:

Will you decide today to take preventive measures so that you can remain in the right place at the right time?

Moment of Silence:

Dear Lord Jesus, I pray that you will draw me close to you and give me determination to stay where I can hear you. You are my lifeline to being directed to the right places in life. I also pray that you will give me tenacity to finish the job that you have called me to. I don't want to wander out of position. Amen.

DAY 2

Moment of Truth:

"But thank God! He has made us his captives and continues to lead us along in Christ's triumphal procession. Now he uses us to spread the knowledge of Christ everywhere, like a sweet perfume." 2 Corinthians 2:14 (NLT)

Moment of Reflection:

Can you retrace how Christ has been leading you from one stepping stone to another?

Take a moment and write down some of your stepping stones.

Moment of Clarity:

For me to be able to write this book, I had to develop a passion to help women. For me to develop that passion, I had to serve my local church. For me to serve my local church, I had to make a commitment. For me to make a commitment, I had to leave the comfort of where I was.

And on and on it goes. I could retrace the stepping stones to my birth, but you get the picture.

God uses our faithfulness and obedience in our current circumstances to position us for more.

He will never give you more than you can handle, but let me assure you, you can handle a whole lot more than you think you can.

With faithfulness and obedience on your current step, you can grow. You can stretch. You can increase your capacity for more. God sees your efforts. He sees your diligence and your authenticity. He longs to give you the desires of your heart. He's just been waiting for you to get in position!

Moment of Decision:

Will you ask God to show you how you can flourish right where you are, on the current stepping stone you are standing on? And then determine to do it with all your might.

Moment of Silence:

Heavenly Father, thank you for the spot I'm standing in. I know I have not always been grateful for it, but there are others who would be happy to be on this stone. Help me to be completely faithful and to live in expectation of the day you move me to the next stone. Amen.

DAY 3

Moment of Truth:

"I have hidden your word in my heart, that I might not sin against you." Psalms 119:11 (NLT)

Moment of Reflection:

Going to church, reading God's word, or loving others - Which one is most difficult for you?

Moment of Clarity:

When we are giving our best efforts to grow, it's hard to know what to invest in more, things that come easy or things that are hard. I have heard arguments expounding the value of playing to your strengths, and I have heard others say we should overcome our weaknesses. I believe it is possible to do both. We can thrive in what we are good at, and possibly help others to get better at it as well. We can also grow in our areas of weakness at the same time. It doesn't have to be one or the other. We can do both.

When Paul was explaining the thorn in his flesh, he asked God to take it away. *"Each time he said, 'My grace is all you need. My power works best in weakness.' So now I am glad to boast about my weaknesses, so that the power of Christ can work through me."* 2 Corinthians 12:9 (NLT)

God is glorified in our strengths and He loves to use them for His kingdom, but He can also be greatly glorified in our weaknesses because they cause us to rely on Him. Whether you find reading the Bible, going to church, or loving others most difficult, you can thrive in them all when you fully rely on the Lord to grow them in you.

Moment of Decision:

Will you strive to become more consistent in these three areas so that you will be positioned for more?

Moment of Silence:

Dear Jesus, I'm sorry for sometimes not obeying you in these basic things that you expect of me. Please forgive me, and help me to begin to thrive in the simple things, so I can be ready for bigger things. Amen.

DAY 4

Moment of Truth:

"Arise, shine, for your light has come, and the glory of the Lord rises upon you." Isaiah 60:1 (NIV)

Moment of Reflection:

Is there a situation or person you are facing that requires you to rise?

Moment of Clarity:

A friend of mine once referred to the difficult people in her life as "sandpaper people." I asked what she meant, and she told me it's because their rough edges actually sand the rough stuff off her. I never forgot that because it made me stop and evaluate what kind of difficulty I was actually facing each time I had an unwanted encounter with someone. (We all have them.)

You might cross paths with very intentional joy-stealing people, or dream-killing people, or attention-sucking people, or you might meet unintentional sandpaper people. You will be wise to know the difference because your response needs to flex appropriately.

The unintentional sandpaper people? Obvious. Just love them and limit your time with them as much as you can. Joy-stealing, dream-killing, attention-sucking people might demand a different response. Yes, we need to love everyone, but that does not mean we should become a doormat to people or allow ourselves to be abused. There might come a time when you need to rise up. Tell them what you need from them, tell them what you will accept, and if it doesn't change, separate yourself from them.

In order for you to find freedom to be who God has called you to be, you need to surround yourself with people who will help position you for greatness.

Moment of Decision:

Will you become more savvy in determining what kind of relationships you have so that you can respond in a way that brings freedom?

Moment of Silence:

Dear God, I pray that you will give me wisdom and courage so that I can move forward in my relationships. I know that you want me to live in freedom, and I thank you for leading me in it. Amen.

DAY 5

Moment of Truth:

"Trust in the Lord with all your heart; do not depend on your own understanding. Seek his will in all you do, and he will show you which path to take." Proverbs 3:5, 6 (NLT)

Moment of Reflection:

When you step into the unknown, are you able to trust God completely?

Moment of Clarity:

When we position ourselves for more from God, we set our lives up for adventure. Some people thrive on adventure, like Bear Grylls dropping out of a helicopter and surviving in the wilderness with no supplies, no food, no nothing. Others of us would be a little reticent to take that leap. Following Bear Grylls would be one thing, but when we follow God, we know He is with us, so we can do anything!

There is an oft quoted saying, "If God brought you to it, He'll bring you through it." I don't know who first said it, but it is true. Everything we go through passes through the hand of our Father first. We can count on Jesus to not only understand what we are going through, but also to have a plan for where He is bringing us. He loves you more than you will ever know, and His plans for you are good.

God's Word is full of promises to encourage us to trust Him more. *"For I can do everything through Christ, who gives me strength."* Philippians 4:13 (NLT) *"The Lord is for me, so I will have no fear. What can mere people do to me?"* Psalm 118:6 (NLT) *"The Lord is my light and my salvation - so why should I be afraid? The Lord is my fortress, protecting me from danger, so why should I tremble?"* Psalm 27:1 (NLT)

Whatever God has positioned you for, you are capable of handling and ready to conquer. David was ready for Goliath because he was faithful in the stepping stones. He positioned himself for greatness, and you can too. You can do all you know to do, you can take responsibility for the people in your world, and you can trust God with the unknown that lies before you.

Moment of Decision:

Will you choose to trust God with all the unknown variables in your life today?

Moment of Silence:

Dear Jesus, I trust in you. You have saved me, changed me, and set me free. I know I can trust you with every detail of my life. Thank you, Lord. Amen.

Chapter 6
Made For Being

UNDERSTANDING OUR value and knowing who we are and what we are made for is a huge accomplishment for us. Doing things to advance the Kingdom of God is what we strive for, and doing things to grow our personal capacity is healthy and exciting. But the truth is, *doing* is just a byproduct of *being*. If we skip this element of *being*, we've missed the whole point!

Saint Augustine said, "Do you wish to be great? Then begin by being. Do you desire to construct a vast and lofty fabric? Think first about the foundations of humility. The higher your structure is to be, the deeper must be its foundation."[1]

Being who God has designed us to be allows us to do great things for God as a natural outflow of who we are. Being with Jesus allows us to reach for a greater destiny. Sometimes people get that backwards. They do and do and do, hoping that that will make them a better person, but it's the other way around. We have to be with Him before we do anything.

When Peter and John began doing ministry, the people were amazed at them. *"The members of the council were amazed when they saw the boldness of Peter and John, for they could see that they were ordinary men with no special training in the Scriptures. They also recognized them as men who had been with Jesus."* Acts 4:13 (NLT) They were able to do mighty things and have great boldness because they had been with Jesus. The *being* always precedes the *doing*.

After God's Own Heart

We have talked a lot about the life of David and all that he did for God. What an unusual leader and man of God he was. The Bible says he was a man after God's own heart. The Bible says,

> *"When David's time to die approached, he charged his son Solomon, saying, 'I'm about to go the way of all the earth, but you-be strong; show what you're made of! Do what God tells you. Walk in the paths he shows you: Follow the life-map absolutely, keep an eye out for the signposts, his course for life set out in the revelation to Moses; then you'll get on well in whatever you do and wherever you go.'"* 1 Kings 2:1-3 (MSG)

This scripture clearly demonstrates why he was a man after God's own heart. He followed closely after God. He had spent time being with God. He was faithfully obedient. He followed the path, step by step. When history recorded his contribution on the earth the words were few, but powerful. *"For David served God's purposes in his own time..."* Acts 13:36 (GNT)

Serving the Purposes of God in Our Time

The desire to serve the purposes of God in my time has been a driving passion in my life, and it has become what drives the women of Our Time as well. We ask questions like, how can we serve God's purposes in our time? What does it mean to be a good servant?

We can more easily identify with a servant by calling them an employee. What makes a good employee? When my husband and I hire an employee for our ministry, we want someone with talent and skill, but we also want someone with heart. We look for a person who is excellent in spirit and in deed. We have learned the hard way that a person who does good work but has no heart is not someone who will go the distance. And a person with all heart and no work ethic is quickly seen as a flake. A good employee must have both skill and heart, and the same can be said for a servant. A good servant has skill and heart; in other words, they *do* and they *be*.

Why is it so hard for us to simply be? I think it's because doing is measurable. Doing is tangible. But being requires a completely different set of skills.

A New Set of Skills

When I was about fourteen years old I went to summer camp. In my church background, summer camp was the place where you'd go to meet with and experience God. I wanted more from God so badly. I had heard speakers and pastors talk about being "filled with the Spirit, with evidence of speaking in tongues"; however, with my shy personality, I was so very afraid of it. I didn't know what effect the Holy Spirit might have on me.

In spite of all my reservations, I was determined to

have more of God. One summer night in a hot, packed-out youth service I had an encounter with God's presence, and I received my prayer language. That prayer language was simply an evidence of the Holy Spirit being active in my life, but what a difference it made!

My parents happened to be camping nearby and the next day I walked to their camp site to say hello. My heart was just gushing! Filled to overflowing! My parents were not there, so I left a note - I didn't tell them what had happened, I just told them how much I loved them.

When I saw my mom at the end of the week, the first thing she said when she saw me, "You got filled with the Holy Spirit, didn't you?" How did she know? You see, my mom was a Christian and she recognized the "signs." My love note was all the evidence she needed to know that I had been changed. I was walking with a new spring in my step. I was loving people with more exuberance.

There are always signs associated with the work of the Holy Spirit.

In the book of Galatians, Paul was writing to the people of Galatia, explaining what the result of a God-lived life would look like. He was describing the evidence, or fruit, of a life that is consecrated to Jesus.

> *"But the Holy Spirit produces this kind of fruit in our lives: love, joy, peace, patience, kindness, goodness, faithfulness, gentleness, and self-control. There is no law against these things! Those who belong to Christ Jesus have nailed the passions and desires of their sinful nature to his cross and crucified them there. Since we are living by the Spirit, let us follow the Spirit's leading in every part of our lives."* Galatians 5:22-25 (NLT)

Being a Woman of Our Time

A Mother's Love

Perhaps there has been no other figure within our recent history who has been more symbolic of love than Mother Teresa. Although she was never a physical mother, she cared for more children than any of us ever will. She said, "I'm a little pencil in the hand of a writing God, who is sending a love letter to the world."

She started *The Missionaries of Charity* which is now a ministry with a worldwide reach, helping feed, clothe, and care for some of the poorest people on earth. In 1979 she was awarded the Nobel Peace Prize. In the press release, it said, "The Committee has placed special emphasis on the spirit that has inspired her activities and which is the tangible expression of her personal attitude and human qualities. A feature of her work has been respect for the individual human being, for his or her dignity and innate value. The loneliest, the most wretched and the dying have, at her hands, received compassion without condescension, based on reverence for man."[2]

They recognized the *spirit that had inspired her activities.* Mother Teresa knew how to love because she had a relationship with God that allowed His Holy Spirit to work in her.

We have that same Spirit in us! When we asked Jesus to be the Lord of our lives, at the moment of salvation, the Holy Spirit took up residence in us! Since He is within us, love is the evidence. *"Your love for one another will prove to the world that you are my disciples."* John 13:35 (NLT)

Joy Unspeakable

I have found His grace is all complete,
He supplieth every need;
While I sit and learn at Jesus' feet,
I am free, yes, free indeed.

Refrain:
It is joy unspeakable and full of glory,
Full of glory, full of glory;
It is joy unspeakable and full of glory,
Oh, the half has never yet been told.

I have found the pleasure I once craved,
It is joy and peace within;
What a wondrous blessing, I am saved
From the awful gulf of sin.
I have found that hope so bright and clear,
Living in the realm of grace;

Oh, the Savior's presence is so near,
I can see His smiling face.
I have found the joy no tongue can tell,
How its waves of glory roll;
It is like a great o'erflowing well,
Springing up within my soul.[3]

Barney E. Warren penned the lyrics to this song in 1900. It

was inspired by 1 Peter 1:8, *"Whom not having known, you love; in whom, though now you don't see him, yet believing, you rejoice greatly with joy unspeakable and full of glory"* 1 Peter 1:8 (WEB)

I grew up singing this old hymn in church. I loved the cadence of the lyrics along with the happy melody, but my favorite line in the song was, "and the half has never yet been told." Even in my child-sized brain, I knew that meant that we don't know it all yet, we don't see it all yet, and no matter how happy I feel right now, there is MORE to come! That was amazing to me!

Now that I am older, I realize that along with times of happiness there are also times of deep sorrow. It is part of us living in a fallen world. The Bible tells us that the rain falls on the just and the unjust. It's not like only a few of us experience these things, we all do! So what gets you through it?

Have you ever watched someone go through a very painful experience with grace and ease and you just had to wonder how on earth they did it?

I have a friend named Mary Ann. She and her husband Glen had been pastors and leaders in Northern California and were greatly admired and loved by thousands of people. They had been married for 58 years. On Valentine's Day this year, her husband went home to be with the Lord. I can't imagine how painful that kind of loss must be for Mary Ann, and yet just a few days after her husband passed away, she stood at the microphone in front of a huge gathering of people.

She stood joyful, smiling, and thankful for all God had given her. She quoted a passage of scripture from Isaiah. *"O Lord, You are my God. O Lord, You are my God. I will exalt You, I will praise Your name, For You have done wonderful things; Your counsels of old are faithfulness and truth."* Isaiah 25:1 (NKJV)

Her life expressed what we all know to be true, the joy of the Lord is our strength. The joy of the Lord is different than happiness. Happiness comes and goes with the circumstances. True unspeakable joy is a joy that sustains us through sorrow, it is a joy that allows us to trust God during uncertainty, and it is a joy that gives us hope for the future.

When we are filled with the Holy Spirit, we can be like the Proverbs 31 woman. *"She is clothed with strength and dignity, and she laughs without fear of the future."* Proverbs 31:25 (NLT) The Holy Spirit produces the fruit of joy in us that is impossible to understand.

Creaky Floors and Bumps in the Night

When I was young, as I have told you, I was quite shy. I was also an extreme worry-wart. Seriously, I think I must've been somewhat neurotic. I was always upset and scared when around people, at school, and in social settings; I would make myself sick worrying. I remember being at home as a young girl, and as the old wooden floors would creak and there were bumps in the night, alone in my bed I would worry about ghosts in my closet, creatures under my bed, "a demon under every bush," so to speak.

I look back now and think how patient my parents must have been with me. Time and time again, they had to soothe their middle child. My mother had exasperated herself trying to talk some sense into me. Finally one night she came in to my room armed with a fantastic weapon. She sat on the edge of my bed and gave me one little scripture verse. One that I memorized and carried with me out of that stage and into every other stage of life.

"For God is not a God of disorder [some versions

say confusion] *but of peace, as in all the meetings of God's holy people."* 1 Corinthians 14:33 (NLT)

I began to understand that anything I was feeling that wasn't producing peace meant that it was not of God. Therefore, I could choose. I could choose to suffer in fear and anxiety or I could choose to pursue peace, to chase it down, and claim it as my own.

You can do that too. The circumstance you face is much more real than a bump in the night, but it's no more difficult for God to manage. He is our all sufficient, omniscient, omnipresent Father! He is the one who said, *"I am leaving you with a gift—peace of mind and heart. And the peace I give is a gift the world cannot give. So don't be troubled or afraid."* John 14:27 (NLT) We need to take that gift of peace and hold on to it every day!

Father Knows Best

We were given this hope when we were saved. *"If we already have something, we don't need to hope for it. But if we look forward to something we don't yet have, we must wait patiently and confidently."* Romans 8:24-25 (NLT) Hmmm...patiently. How good are you at waiting?

Patience. The cold hard edges of this word written on the page are one thing, but accepting the harsh reality of it in real life, is another. Maybe you can relate. When I pray I want answers! I want results!

Everything about God says that He is strategic. He's not an accidental God. He created us on purpose. His plans for us are intentional. His timing is perfect. Therefore, we should trust Him. Right? The funny thing is, even though we know all of these things, it doesn't make it easier to have patience.

One night while frustrated, I was praying for the same thing yet again, seeing very little affect of my pleas again, crying out to God again, stomping around the sanctuary of our church as I often do, pouring my heart out to God. Stopped in my tracks, I felt God whisper one word into my spirit.

Surrender. It was a sudden, unwanted discovery! Patience requires something of me that is most challenging to give.

I immediately hit my knees. I had to ask forgiveness for pouting and crying like a child, demanding my own way. After all, I thought that I was way past that toddler like behavior! I was a mature woman of God, for Pete's sake! Didn't God know what was best for me? Didn't He know how important this was to me?

Maybe you've felt that way. Patiently waiting on God to act is tricky. You can't go by how you feel because emotions are fickle. You have to rely on the truth of God's reality. Matthew Henry wrote, "Cast not away your confidence because God defers his performances. That which does not come in your time, will be hastened in his time, which is always the more convenient season. God will work when he pleases, how he pleases, and by what means he pleases. He is not bound to keep our time, but he will perform his word, honor our faith, and reward them that diligently seek him."

God does know. He knows how important you are to Him, and how important it is that you grow up. He knows how important it is that you are trusting Him and being confident in Him.

Patience requires surrender. Surrender of our preconceived ideas, surrender of our need to control, surrender of our timetable, surrender of our desires and wishes to His. "...we must wait patiently and confidently."

The Sweet Smell of Jesus

My youngest son Greyson has had a transformation take place in His life. God dramatically got ahold of his heart and he is truly not the same as he was before. The rebellious, angry, hostile, boy he was at eighteen is not the young man he is at nineteen. I had never witnessed anything like it before in my life. (And frankly, I wouldn't have believed it could be possible if I hadn't seen it with my own two eyes.)

He spends hours in his room at night reading the Bible and praying. He listens to worship music all day long as he works and drives to school. He tells people about Jesus every chance he gets. Greyson is living proof of the evidence of spending time in the presence of the Lord. His life overflows with the fruits of the Spirit. Kindness and goodness have become not what he *does*, but who he *is*.

One day as he was on his way to work, he passed a homeless man holding a cardboard sign in the supermarket parking lot. He circled back around and went and talked to the man. The man said his name was Michael. Greyson handed Michael some money, but he also gave him more than money. He handed him hope that day. He asked him how he was, asked if he was hurting, and listened to Michael share his disappointment with life. Greyson explained that God loves him so much and has a plan for his life that is good. He stood right there, on the edge of the busy parking lot, laid hands on Michael and asked God for healing and restoration and hope for him.

That is the fruit of the Spirit pouring out of a person sold out for the cause of Christ. I want to be more like that. I need more of that! 2 Corinthians 2:15 says, "*Because of Christ, we give off a sweet scent rising to God, which is recognized by those on the way of salvation-an aroma redolent with life."* (MSG)

I want the fruit of the Spirit's kindness and goodness to ooze out of me like grape jelly! Leaving a sweet smell on everything I touch.

No Sister Alone

No Sister Alone

My husband was a Navy Chaplain but served the Marine Corps for many years. I worked very closely with the military wives, especially during times of deployment. We became a sisterhood that mirrored the beliefs of the men we supported. Semper Fi - Always Faithful. If one wife needed help with her kids, there was always another wife who would step in. I loved that, I lived that, and it became a part of who I am.

The women of Our Time have developed a code of ethics when it comes to our relationships, as well. We have become a sisterhood. Psalm 68:6 says, *"God places the lonely in families; he sets the prisoners free and gives them joy..."* (NLT) I believe that those "families" are found within the context of the local church. We faithfully choose to be family to one another. If one sister is hurting, other sisters gather around and give comfort. If one sister is rejoicing, other sisters throw a party and we celebrate together. If one sister goes to the altar, she doesn't go alone. If one sister shouts, she doesn't shout alone.

We express faithfulness by reflecting loyalty to our sisters. Only truly knowing Jesus and allowing the Holy Spirit to fill us can give us faithfulness like that.

Power Under Control

I have a friend who teaches a morning Bible study for women at our church. She patiently unpacks the treasures from the Word of God and mentors women every week.

I have a friend who ministers daily to her neighbors, and so attractive is her faith that she often has a whole row of neighborhood disciples sitting with her on Sunday mornings.

I have a friend who teaches a very popular quilting class every week which caters to women of all backgrounds and faiths, and sometimes to those with no faith at all. She cares for them so beautifully that when she opens up her home to host all day quilt camps they want to sleep over! They have so much fun together.

I have a friend who has served as the very first female member of our board of deacons at Capital Christian Center. She is an example that there is no separation between male and female leadership calling in the kingdom of God.

I have a friend who humbly serves at our city's hospital, running the gift shop for the Auxiliary group.

Would you believe these examples are all one woman? She

is my 80-year-old friend, Margaret. I call her MargaROCK, because she does! She is amazing! She rocks! Her ability, capacity, energy, and knowledge are things many of us aspire to. But she is always humble, considering the needs and hurts of others before considering herself. In my dictionary, if you look up the definition of gentleness, you would see a picture of Margaret.

When the Greeks originally wrote the New Testament, they defined gentleness as "power under control."[4] When we have spent time being with Jesus, He empowers us to be humble, and to harness our own ambition as we serve others. We can be gentle because Jesus was gentle.

The cross is the ultimate picture of power under control. Jesus could have chosen to exert His strength and authority, but He chose to put us first. When we allow the Holy Spirit to work in us, we can become a reflection of the gentleness of Jesus.

Stronger Than Willpower

Seventeen months ago, I set a new dietary goal. I decided that I would not eat meat or any animal byproducts or refined sugar or flour for six weeks. I wanted to get healthier. I have suffered from migraine headaches, as well as allergies for years. I read that a vegan diet could greatly improve things. So I set my mind to it.

I mustered the willpower and I was determined, but I found out real fast that I have a weakness for certain things. Things like cheese. And bread. And comfort foods like mashed potatoes and gravy. And cake. I had to reach deeper than my own willpower could go.

Many addicts spend most of their lives trying to get better. But when they try to do better based on their own willpower, they quickly discover that their willpower isn't very strong at all. Depending on the level of temptation, results vary.

When we invite God in, surrender our life to Him, and really begin to know Him, it changes everything. We find out that willpower is not our strongest ally, self control is! Self-control is not man-made. We don't manufacture self-control; it is a fruit of the Holy Spirit.

> *"There's a struggle going on inside of us — a fight for control. Our willpower fails us repeatedly. Where can we turn when we can't get control of our life? The apostle Paul said to the Galatians, 'The Holy Spirit produces this kind of fruit in our lives: love, joy, peace, patience, kindness, goodness, faithfulness, gentleness, and self-control.'"* Galatians 5:22-23 (The Life Recovery Bible[5]).

Spending time in the presence of Jesus fills us with His Holy Spirit, and He gives us power to do anything! No addiction or weakness is stronger than our God! What we are made of is pretty tough stuff. I can now say I have been a vegan for seventeen months, thanks to the Holy Spirit filling me up; I realize it's not about my own willpower, but it's about His power giving me self-control.

The nine fruits of the Spirit make us into a beautiful reflection of Jesus, and not because we've earned it. It's not because we deserve it or by anything we've done. We bear fruit simply by *being* with Him.

The Secret is In the Secret

I am just now learning how to *be* with Him. When I was younger, I thought Luke 8:17 was a threat. It says, *"For all that is secret will eventually be brought into the open, and everything that is concealed will be brought to light and made known to all."* (NLT) I remember a well-intentioned, finger-wagging Sunday School teacher using this scripture to remind us that nothing is hidden from the Lord's sight and that all our actions will someday be judged. All of that is true, but as I am growing in my relationship with the Lord, I now see this verse as more of a promise.

I believe all the hidden time we spend studying God's Word works itself out in the light of our everyday life. I believe that all the secret hours we spend in prayer are not wasted. On the contrary, they are stored up as investments that pay dividends in daily blessings and provide us victory after victory. I believe spending time with Jesus changes our countenance, our outlook, and our expectation. The secret place is our secret to a life filled with the power of the Holy Spirit.

We sometimes pull away from spending time with Jesus because we think the cost will be too high. We resist His call because we believe we have too much to lose, but in reality, we have everything to gain.

> *"He who dwells in the secret place of the Most High shall remain stable and fixed under the shadow of the Almighty [Whose power no foe can withstand]."* Psalm 91:1 (AMP)

Invincible

Being with Him is how we discover what we're made of, and what we're made of is not us at all! We are made of all the goodness that He is. His very breath and Spirit reside within us. When we learn to *be* with Him, we are surprised to find that our strength is not dependent upon us but upon Him. Our sufficiency is not ours; it is God's. All the things we *do* for Him are just the residual evidence of having *been* with Him.

We no longer have to be afraid of what He sees in our performance when we understand that He simply wants to be with us. When He looks at us He doesn't see our lack, he sees our potential. He doesn't see our sin; he sees his blood and the victory that it bought. He doesn't see our stains; He sees His purity as we are washed white as snow. He doesn't see our flaws; He sees His grace.

How long will we wait to take our place? He has called us. He has appointed us. He has anointed us. He has positioned us. He has equipped us. And yet we sit and wait? What are we waiting for? Someone else? Someone more qualified? The next generation? Let the waiting end today. Let us be a generation of women who will rise and take our rightful place.

> *"On your feet, Daughter of Zion! Be threshed of chaff, be refined of dross. I'm remaking you into a people invincible."* Micah 4:13 (MSG)

He is remaking us into a people invincible! Don't you love that? Women of God, I charge you. Your time is now! Rise up. Be bold. Be strong. Take courage. You were made for this moment.

Brenda's Story
In Her Own Words

Before I was born, a thread was established in my family to serve God. My sweet Grandma was a prayer warrior and worked hard to raise two boys after losing another son and her husband to disease. My dad was about as perfect as a human could be and walked closely with God. My heritage is one of trusting God no matter what. He is always faithful.

My mother died when I was six from a painful battle with cancer. God was faithful. Fast forward to high school graduation and the beginning of dreams for what my future held. At a youth retreat I had the most amazing encounter with God and knew I was called to a life of ministry and service. I began on a foreign mission assignment for a year and learned God's love and faithfulness on my own for the first time.

As a young woman I was quite shy, very naive and trusting. I met a man at church. He exhibited a desire to be a godly leader, and he told me that "God told him we were to be married" the first time he saw me. Well, I was naive enough to believe that if GOD said it, it must be what He wanted for my life.

We married one and a half years later. We shared wedded bliss and great family moments and two fabulous kids for eighteen years. Happiness was interrupted often. I was controlled and treated as an object rather than a wife. Self-love and the love of things to make him look successful became all-consuming in his life. We were the "nice family": a wife and two kids behind the proverbial picket fence as trophies to an empire.

During these years while often alone, I spent my time at church with the kids. It was during those years God was beginning to develop me into His design. I learned leadership by working with the children's programs and was shoved out of my comfort zone as I was a part of the women's ministry leadership team.

I remember one day sitting on the porch of my 5,000-square-foot home that was set in a beautiful location and watching my two kids play, thinking, "I really have a great life." But I wasn't happy. A few weeks later my world crumbled as I learned that my husband had been living a double life and had been unfaithful the entire time we were married.

I was strong but I was devastated. I knew I had to take care of my kids and live for our future, but I didn't want to go through what I had to face. I wanted to escape. My family and a few friends gave me the support I needed. I'm not a huge fan of TV evangelists, but I tuned in one night and they were singing a song and it went like this: "God will take care of you, in every way and all the way, God will take care of you! He will take care of you." They sang that for 45 minutes over and over and finally the preacher came on and said, "That wasn't planned. I'm supposed to preach, but I believe that was for someone." I grabbed it! It was for me! It was His promise to take care of me, and He has taken care of me every step from that moment on. God is faithful.

God continues to mold me. There have been times where I haven't been as in tune to His voice, but I have never looked back. My Dad died two years ago, and he told me before he died that he had been called to be a preacher but he was never able to pursue it. At that moment I knew that my call to a life of ministry was a part of my Dad's calling as well, a part of a tapestry.

The past two years I have been running after God and listening like never before in my life for the call of my next chapter. My life has been transformed, and I'm being made into His image to be used. I hear His voice; I have learned to be obedient and trust. I have never stopped serving Him, but now it has become a passion. All that I have experienced in life has led me to where I am today and these moments. My life is His, and I am happy.

This year I have begun a new ministry through Our Time. God is asking me to love women who are often judged, despised, thrown out as trash, and controlled, and who live a life without worth. The name of this new ministry is Xquisite, and it will serve to demonstrate to these women that they are stunning, cherished, and priceless because that is how God views them. I have been training for this moment, and God has always been faithful. It is time and I am ready.

Defining Moments In Your Day

DAY 1

Moment of Truth:

"Let be and be still, and know (recognize and understand) that I am God. I will be exalted among the nations! I will be exalted in the earth!" Psalm 46:10 (AMP)

Moment of Reflection:

Is it difficult for you to shift gears from *doing* for God to *being* with God?

Moment of Clarity:

This is a problem that women have faced for over 2,000 years. Jesus addressed it openly with his friends Mary and Martha. Jesus was teaching the people while staying at the home of Mary, Martha, and their brother Lazarus. While Jesus was teaching, Martha was in the kitchen preparing food and working hard to be a great hostess. Meanwhile, her sister Mary was just sitting at Jesus' feet, listening intently.

Martha got so mad she actually brought the problem to Jesus' attention. She fumed, "I'm doing all this stuff, and Mary is just sitting there! Tell her, Jesus, tell her to get up and help me!"

"But the Lord said to her, 'My dear Martha, you are worried and upset over all these details! There is only one thing worth being concerned about. Mary has discovered it, and it will not be taken away from her.'" Luke 10:41-42 (NLT)

Jesus said stop *doing* and start *being*! Have you ever been too concerned about the wrong things that made you forfeit being with Jesus?

Moment of Decision:

Will you make a fresh commitment today to spend more time being with the Savior?

Moment of Silence:

Dear Jesus, please help me to make a new habit of simply spending time being with you. I need you to invade my busy world and show me who you are. Amen.

DAY 2

Moment of Truth:

"Even before he made the world, God loved us and chose us in Christ to be holy and without fault in his eyes." Ephesians 1:4 (NLT)

Moment of Reflection:

Name a person who fits this description: He/She is serving the purposes of God in our time. Why do you think so?

Moment of Clarity:

Christine Caine[6] is an example of a woman who serves the purposes of God in our time.

She travels the globe preaching to people about their potential and their destiny and the love of Jesus Christ. She preaches the Word of God with fire and with passion. Many thousands have come to a relationship with God through her ministry. But she didn't stop there. As she traveled, she saw a very dark and daunting human need. Human trafficking is a problem common to every nation on earth and it seems too big for any one person to make a difference. But Christine is making a difference.

Her A21 Campaign not only brings awareness, it brings justice. She now has attorneys who prosecute those responsible for human trafficking. She has homes for girls who are rescued from prostitution. She is making a very big dent in this issue in countries all over the world, all because her love and passion for Jesus spilled out as love for others.

Christine's story could've easily turned out differently. She was raised in Australia by Greek parents. But one day a piece of paper came in the mail that told her she had been unwanted, unnamed, and discarded as an infant. She could've become a victim, but she didn't. Christine found the unconditional love of a Savior, and she found the security of a church family that cared enough about her to grow her and give her a chance. Because she has been set free by Jesus, she is now setting others free.

She spent many years *being* before she spent any time *doing*. She let God heal her and make her whole before she got busy serving Him. We all need that. We need to allow God to heal us of past issues and hurts; we need to sit at His feet and let His words wash over us until we are filled to overflowing. It is in the overflow that we truly serve God's purposes in our time.

Moment of Decision:

What do you still need to have Jesus heal before you begin to serve? Have you sat at His feet long enough?

Moment of Silence:

Dear Lord, I pray that you will heal the wounds of my past. I pray that you will remove the sting of rejection and past pain and fill me up with the knowledge that you love me. Unconditionally. Right now. Just as I am. Thank you Jesus, for accepting me. Amen.

DAY 3

Moment of Truth:

"But you will receive power when the Holy Spirit comes upon you. And you will be my witnesses, telling people about me everywhere—in Jerusalem, throughout Judea, in Samaria, and to the ends of the earth." Acts 1:8 (NLT)

Moment of Reflection:

Do you feel the power of the Holy Spirit at work in you?

Moment of Clarity:

When we accept Jesus as our Savior, He comes into our hearts and He brings everything He is with Him. We must understand that it is no small thing to have God's power at work within us. We can choose to acknowledge and use what He has given us, or we can deny His power entirely.

There are a lot of weak Christians in the world who walk through life defeated and living in fear simply because they don't recognize the gift that is in them! 2 Timothy 3:5 describes them like this, *"They will act religious, but they will reject the power that could make them godly. Stay away from people like that!"* (NLT)

I don't want to *act* like a Christian; I want to really *be* one! Because of what Jesus accomplished on the cross for us, we not only have salvation, we have true freedom! We have direct access to God! All the power that is in the Holy Spirit is in us. We are not weak - we are strong! We are not defeated - we are victorious! We are not sick and anemic - we are made whole! We are not dead - we are alive in Christ!

"But you belong to God, my dear children. You have already won a victory over those people, because the Spirit who lives in you is greater than the spirit who lives in the world." 1 John 4:4 (NLT)

Moment of Decision:

How might you acknowledge the Spirit of God within you by how you live?

Moment of Silence:

Dear Heavenly Father, thank you for taking up residency in my life. I want to begin to believe it, to know that your power is real, and to walk in a manner worthy of your grace in my life. Teach me how. Amen.

DAY 4

Moment of Truth:

"But the Holy Spirit produces this kind of fruit in our lives: love, joy, peace, patience, kindness, goodness, faithfulness, gentleness, and self-control." Galatians 5:22 (NLT)

Moment of Reflection:

Of the fruits of the Spirit, is there one that seems to be more active in you than the others? Which one is it?

Moment of Clarity:

In all honesty, we have the ability to push ourselves and make ourselves behave better if we really work hard at it. There are a lot of really nice people out there who think they will get to go to heaven simply because they're a good person. But we know that good works aren't enough to get us into heaven. Good works aren't even enough to get God's favor or to get Him to love us any more. His gifts of grace and favor are simply part of the deep well that is God's love for us.

"For it is by free grace (God's unmerited favor) that you are saved (delivered from judgment and made partakers of Christ's salvation) through [your] faith. And this [salvation] is not of yourselves [of your own doing, it came not through your own striving], but it is the gift of God" Ephesians 2:8 (AMP)

It is so difficult for us to understand that there is nothing we can do to get Him to love us more. Not if we read the Bible more, not if we hold our tongue more frequently, not if we don't get even with people. Jesus simply loves us. Right now! In the condition we are in. He just loves us!

We also have this thought that when Jesus gave up His life on the cross, he did it to redeem all of mankind. We put all humanity in a group. Somehow we can justify that enormous sacrifice he made when the group is large enough. It removes the sting of guilt a little when we are lumped together. But that isn't the whole truth. Jesus died for you. Individually. Just you! As if you were the only one. To him, you were worth it. Saint Augustine wrote, "God loves each of us as if there were only one of us." He loves us just as we are, but thankfully He doesn't leave us as we are.

Amazing grace, how sweet the sound, that saved an insecure, weak, addicted, lost, wounded, scared girl like me. Insert whatever adjectives that fit, but He still loves you just the same! I once was lost but now I'm found, was blind, but now I see.

Moment of Decision:

Will you simply rest on His grace and favor today?

Moment of Silence:

Dear God, thank you for loving me. Help me to comprehend it and rest in it. I am amazed by You. I love you, Jesus. Amen

DAY 5

Moment of Truth:

"Hang my locket around your neck, wear my ring on your finger. Love is invincible facing danger and death. Passion laughs at the terrors of hell. The fire of love stops at nothing-it sweeps everything before it." Song of Solomon 8:6 (MSG)

Moment of Reflection:

What does "invincible" mean to you?

Moment of Clarity:

The commentator Matthew Henry[7] explains that the Song of Solomon is written as an allegory, drawing comparisons between Christ and His bride, the Church. It describes His passion for us in vivid detail. His love for us is invincible.

Against all opposition, His love prevails. Hell couldn't conquer His love for us, and there is nothing we can do to push away or destroy His love for us either. It is invincible.

Merriam-Webster[8] defines invincible as "incapable of being conquered, overcome or subdued." I love that the passage of scripture in Micah 4:13 in the Message Bible says, *"On your feet, Daughter of Zion! ...I'm remaking you into a people invincible."*

We are people who are unstoppable because God's love is limitless! We cannot be overcome because His power is at work within us! No power on earth can hold us down because He lives with us. We must begin to accept what He has done for us, and who He has made us to be. God has set us apart as His own "people invincible"! We were made for this moment!

Moment of Decision:

Will you walk in confidence today, knowing that nothing can stop you?

Moment of Silence:

Dear Lord, thank you for entrusting me with your very presence and power. Help me to live in a way that reflects you to the world. Amen.

It doesn't take long to form new habits, and you have just formed a big one! I congratulate you!

But don't stop now, keep growing, keep stretching, and keep praying. God has got big plans for you. This is your story, write it well. This is your time, make it count. This is your life, live it to the fullest. This is your legacy, make it incredible. You were made for this moment!

Notes

Chapter and Week 1

1. "Abortion Information You Can Use..." *Survivors of Abortion*. N.p., n.d. Web. 20 June 2012.

2. "Pneuma - Greek Lexicon." *Pneuma - Greek Lexicon*. N.p., n.d. Web. 20 June 2012.

3. Vine, W. E., Merrill F. Unger, and William White. *Vine's Complete Expository Dictionary of Old and New Testament Words: With Topical Index*. Nashville: T. Nelson, 1996. Print. Volume 2, 149

4. "Jason Gray - The Sound Of Our Breathing Lyrics." *SongLyrics.com*. N.p., n.d. Web. 20 June 2012.

5. "John Mayer Why Georgia Lyrics." *WHY GEORGIA Lyrics*. N.p., n.d. Web. 20 June 2012.

6. Rick Warren. *Purpose Driven Life* (Grand Rapids, MI: Zondervan, 2002) Print.

7. Williamson, Marianne. *A Return to Love: Reflections on the Principles of a Course in Miracles*. New York, NY: HarperCollins, 1992. Print.

8. W.E. Vine Volume 4, 64

9. Houston, Brian. *For This Cause; Finding the Meaning of Life and Living a Life of Meaning.* Castle Hill, Austalia: Maximised Leadership, 2001. Print.

Chapter and Week 2

1. "God Loves Women Too,Â Right?" *Rumblings.* N.p., n.d. Web. 20 June 2012.
2. "American Rhetoric: Hillary Rodham Clinton -- United Nations 4th World Conference Speech ("Women's Rights Are Human Rights")." *American Rhetoric: Hillary Rodham Clinton -- United Nations 4th World Conference Speech ("Women's Rights Are Human Rights").* N.p., n.d. Web. 20 June 2012.
3. Hedlun, Randy, Gary B. McGee, and Annette Newberry. Assemblies of God History, Missions and Governance. 5th ed. Vol. 1. Springfield: Gospel House, 2010. Print. 3.2, 3.3.

Chapter and Week 3

1. "Katharine Hepburn." *The John F. Kennedy Center for the Performing Arts.* N.p., n.d. Web. 20 June 2012.
2. Gladwell, Malcolm. *Outliers: The Story of Success.* New York: Little, Brown and, 2008. Print.
3. "Top 10 Late Bloomers: Why Age Does Not Matter When It Comes to Success." *Top 10 Late Bloomers: Why Age Does Not Matter When It Comes to Success.* N.p., n.d. Web. 20 June 2012.
4. "Wilbur Wright's Biography." *Wilbur Wright's Biography.* N.p., n.d. Web. 21 June 2012.

Chapter and Week 4

1. PBS. PBS, n.d. Web. 21 June 2012.
2. "Strong's Hebrew: 4609. (ma'alah) -- Step." Strong's Hebrew: 4609. (ma'alah). N.p., n.d. Web. 20 June 2012.
3. "Can a Christian Get a Tattoo?" YouTube. YouTube, 12 Apr. 2010. Web. 21 June 2012.
4. "Praying Circles Around Your Biggest Dreams and Greatest Fears." The Circle Maker. N.p., n.d. Web. 21 June 2012. Print.

Chapter and Week 5

1. BrainyQuote. Xplore, n.d. Web. 12 July 2012.

Chapter and Week 6

1. BrainyQuote. Xplore, n.d. Web. 21 June 2012.
2. "The Nobel Peace Prize 1979." Press Release -. N.p., n.d. Web. 21 June 2012.
3. "JOY UNSPEAKABLE Chords." - BARNEY E. WARREN (Praise and Worship Lyrics & Chords by Higher Praise). N.p., n.d. Web. 21 June 2012.
4. "Matthew 5:5 Commentary." Matthew 5:5 Commentary. N.p., n.d. Web. 21 June 2012.
5. The Life Recovery Bible. [S.l.]: Tyndale House, 1992. Print.
6. "Welcome to the A21 Campaign." Welcome to the A21 Campaign. N.p., n.d. Web. 21 June 2012.
7. "Bible Commentary." Matthew Henryâs Commentary -. N.p., n.d. Web. 21 June 2012.

8. "Invincible." *Merriam-Webster.* Merriam-Webster, n.d. Web. 21 June 2012.

Other Works Cited:

Holy Bible: English Standard Version. Wheaton, IL: Crossway Bibles, 2001. Print.

Holy Bible: Good News Translation. Grand Rapids, MI: Zondervan, 2001. Print.

Holy Bible: New International Version. Grand Rapids, MI: Zondervan, 1984. Print.

Holy Bible: New King James Version. Nashville: T. Nelson, 1990. Print.

Holy Bible: New Living Translation. Wheaton, IL: Tyndale House, 1996. Print.

Peterson, Eugene H. The Message. Colorado Springs, CO: NavPress, 2004. Print.